Searching for God

The Longest Step

The Encounter Series

Searching for God

The Longest Step

James DiGiacomo, S.J.
John Walsh, M.M.

Winston Press

Acknowledgments

Scripture texts (except for 1
Cor.13:12) used in this work are taken
from the NEW AMERICAN BIBLE,
copyright © 1970, by the
Confraternity of Christian Doctrine,
Washington, D.C. All rights reserved.

1 Cor. 13:12 was taken from the *Good
News Bible*, copyright © American
Bible Society 1966, 1971, 1976.

© 1977 by Winston Press, Inc.
Library of Congress Catalog Card Number: 77-72547
ISBN: 0-03-021276-6
Printed in the United States of America

Nihil Obstat: David A. Dillon
Imprimatur: + John R. Roach
            Archbishop of St. Paul and Minneapolis
            March 22, 1977

Contents

1. **Let's start over**   **1**
   Is God a blue elephant?

2. **Don't just sit there**   **13**
   God is a little red-headed girl

3. **We're moving!**   **21**
   The best is yet to come

4. **Going my way?**   **33**
   Meeting God and others

5. **Getting to know you**   **47**
   People who need people

6. **Repairs**   **57**
   What to do when things go wrong

7. **Detour**   **71**
   God is not a blob

8. **On our way**   **83**
   Face to face

   Epilogue   **93**

A journey of a thousand miles begins with a single step.

— Old Chinese saying

The first step is the longest.

— Old saying we just made up

Yes, you may take one giant step.

— Children's game

CHAPTER 1

Let's Start Over

IS GOD A BLUE ELEPHANT?

Which of these two tourists would you rather be at this moment?

Bill is halfway across the Atlantic with a tour group, flying from New York to Paris for a month's vacation. He's never been to Europe, so he ought to feel pretty excited. But he's wondering. This was the best tour the travel agency offered. Mom and Dad thought the tour would be a fine thing. Travel's broadening. You'll see all the sights, meet nice people, have lots of fun. And no worry about hotels, meals, what to do, where to go—it's all taken care of for you.

Bill's thinking. Maybe Hawaii would be a lot better. Some of his buddies have been there, and they loved it. Waving palm trees, sandy beaches, surfing . . . .

But the plane drones on toward Paris.

Joan is at her home in Chicago, studying travel brochures on western Europe and Hawaii. It's agony trying to decide where to go this year, but it's satisfying to plan your own trip.

Maybe you'd like to be in Bill's spot. The stewardess has just told you to fasten your seat belt—the plane's about to land in Paris. In a couple of hours a whole new fascinating world will open up for you. Paris . . . Rome . . . Madrid . . . London. Best of all, no fuss, no muss—it's all taken care of for you. And poor old Joan's stuck in Chicago, biting her nails. Hawaii, or western Europe? Which airline? How will she get around once she arrives? Which hotels? What to see and do?

Or maybe you'd rather be Joan. Despite all the hassle, at least you're going to make up your own mind. Maybe the decision won't be the best, but it'll be yours. You don't like to have someone else make up your mind for you. You prefer to be in charge of your own life.

So who would you rather be—this minute?

It all depends on where and how you want to go.

Is this any way to run a vacation?

Whose idea was this trip, anyway?

Bill and Joan aren't completely fictitious characters.

If we look at the Church in America today, we find many people like Bill. Baptized as infants, they find themselves incorporated into a Christian organization from their earliest years. But now, in their teens, 20s, 30s, 40s or middle age, they're asking themselves, Is there a God? Why do I need a church? What's life all about? Where am I going? What will happen when I die? They're experiencing a basic person-crisis in encountering God, other people, and themselves. They're in a plane called Church on a trip called Religion, and they're not sure if they want to stay on or get off. They're not even clear about how they got on the plane.

On the other hand, if we go to a missionary country like Japan, we meet many people like Joan. Many Japanese arrive at Baptism and Christianity only as teenagers or in their adult life after a long, hard search. These people have had a great deal of experience in dealing with personal problems and crises. On their way to Christianity they've stumbled, fallen, been confused, lost, afraid, angry, and hurt. For such persons, faith comes at the end of a long, twisting road. Like Joan, they keep their options open all the way until the moment of personal decision.

There's no guarantee that Joan's trip will turn out better than Bill's. There's no assurance that the lonely, adult searcher after God will find him and that the one who was carried to church in mother's arms won't. But many people would rather do it Joan's way. Maybe you're one of them.

If you are, this book is for you.

What lies ahead for you if you somehow manage to turn the plane around and start over, this time making your own decision, like Joan? No one can guarantee that you'll find God or others or even yourself. But like good travel agents, we can offer you a brochure that describes, from observation and experience, what has happened to others who took the trip. Allowing for many variations in individual cases, we can describe a typical case history that includes ten stages or steps. Without trying to box in either you or God, let us describe for you these ten stages of experience that we have seen many people pass through on the way to Christian faith. We'll call our typical traveler Dave.

Stage 1

At first, for all practical purposes, Dave doesn't believe in God. Maybe God exists, maybe he doesn't. It's really not that important in daily life. If God does exist, he may be one or many gods. Again, if he does exist, he's way out there—out of the swing of things. He's more of a cosmic force than a personal god. Although Dave may concede that God exists, his gut feeling is that it doesn't really matter one way or the other. It's like the worldwide controversy that rages when someone in Africa reports seeing a blue elephant. Is there really a blue elephant? Maybe. Maybe not. Does it really matter? Maybe God is a blue elephant who doesn't make any difference one way or the other.

With regard to other people, Dave at this stage may have various attitudes. On the one hand, he may have some real friends with whom he experiences good, satisfying relationships. So he wonders, Isn't that enough? Should I be content, instead of restlessly searching beyond for God? On the other hand, he may find himself surrounded by people, yet dying of loneliness. Maybe he lives in a highly structured society, belongs to many groups, is in constant contact with people. He has many acquaintances in family, school, neighborhood, and at work. He knows everybody, yet knows no one. Everybody knows him, yet no one knows him. Acquaintances, yes. Real friendship—a deep personal relationship with someone—no. Surrounded by people, and all alone.

At this stage he may not like himself, either. His self-image may be quite negative. True, many people are painfully aware of certain defects in their own character, but this is much more serious. Perhaps he doesn't care for the person he sees in the mirror. He may sometimes be uncomfortable in his own presence.

His attitude toward religion is even more negative. Religion is for little old ladies; it keeps them off the streets. Religion seems a thing of the past; it smacks of superstition. It's out-dated; it has no place in the modern world. It's a business, a money-making outfit. It's for losers. If you can't cope with life, take refuge in religion, the big band-aid in the sky.

He feels that if he goes near a church, his freedom will be threatened. He's been manipulated time and again by various groups, and he's sure it will happen again. When the forcing is done, there will be a velvet glove; everything will be smooth; no need for shouting. But under the velvet glove there will be an iron fist. He feels in his heart that he will be gently, but firmly, conned into becoming a Christian.

Stage 2
Dave becomes a seeking person. He still doesn't have a clue to what life is all about, but he's looking. The search may take various forms. Maybe he's consciously searching for God. Or he's trying to break out of the prison of his own self and go out to other people, looking for friendship, looking for love. Or maybe he's just trying to find himself. Whatever shape it takes, to go from Stage 1 to Stage 2 is tremendous progress. It may or may not be dramatic, but he has taken a giant step. Maybe the longest step.

Stage 3
In Stage 3, Dave acknowledges that there is a higher Being (God, if you will). He acknowledges that he should encounter God and other people. He's beginning to see that the search for himself, for other people, and for God is somehow all wrapped up together . . . that he can't find one without the others. He admits it in his mind, but he doesn't *do* anything about it. All theory, no action. He acknowledges that as an individual he has worth, but he still feels blah about himself. He admits he needs others, but he hasn't made a move toward them. He senses the need for God, but he hasn't taken that first long step.

Stage 4
He now translates theory into action. He gets off the starting blocks and makes a real effort to encounter God, others, self. This is a real breakthrough, and now all kinds of possibilities open up. For he's not just *thinking* or *talking*; he's *doing*. For the most part he's relying on his own insights and strength alone to carry this out. He feels that if anything is going to happen, *he* must make it happen. *He* must find himself; *he* must find a way to encounter others; *he* must search out God, wherever he's hiding, and bring him out into the open.

Stage 5
Finally comes the day when Dave realizes that he can't hack it all by himself. He's spinning his wheels, going in circles. Gradually he has come to realize, not in theory but by experience, that he needs God's help.

This realization comes to Dave the way it usually does—through a response to God's self-revelation in Scripture. He now sees the Bible, not as literature, not as an ethics book, not as a collection of warm sayings by some nice guy who got zapped two thousand years ago—but as the word of God addressed to him to help him find out what life is all about. He may not understand a word of Scripture at this time. It may all be very confusing. He may get a headache every time he reads it. No matter. It's his basic attitude that counts, and the fact that *he's no longer alone*.

Stage 6
At this stage Dave has a great insight—a great enlightenment, a great breakthrough. Generally, if you seek a great enlightenment you're supposed to go up into the mountains and meditate for about 20 years, just as a preliminary. But there are enlightenments and there are enlightenments. This one can come any place at any time—in a factory, or waiting for a bus, when you're walking or studying. It comes to Dave one day when he's sitting out under an oak tree, daydreaming. He says to himself, as if hearing it for the first time, *God really became one of us!* And he tells himself, I've looked for this insight, but now I know it's a gift. I've worked for it, but all my spiritual weight-lifting couldn't give it to me.

Suddenly Dave knows that God is not some vague something on a cloud ten million miles away. To encounter me, he says wonderingly, God made the greatest leap of all time: he became one of us. Now I know how to understand God—I just look at myself. Do I get tired? Christ got tired. Do I get lonely? Christ was lonely. Do I hurt? Christ hurt. Do I want to be loved? So did Christ. Do I feel like copping out at times? Christ likewise. Do I want to love? He did, too.

Stage 7
When Dave reaches Stage 7, he sees Baptism not merely as a ceremony, a formality that's traditional and therefore expected. It's not just "the thing to do"; it's something *he wants* to do. It's an encounter with Christ and others. Through this sacrament, he accepts God's offer of new life and freely enters into a covenant with Christ in his Church. He pledges himself to believe in him, to live by his values, and to work out his salvation with others who, like him, have accepted Christ's offer of friendship and his gift of love.

Stage 8
Dave now enters into the Christian experience of life. As part of a community trying to live up to its Christian commitment, he worships and prays. He continues to study and to learn. Other Christians help him in time of need and sorrow; when they need him, he reaches out a helping hand. Of course, there are troubles, too. He finds out that people are human, that they have faults. They fail to live up to Christ's ideals. If he's honest, he sees these failings in himself, too. Through these ups and downs, he experiences what the life of a Christian is—not a rose garden, but a rocky path that leads to exciting possibilities.

Stage 9
He now explores the immense possibilities of the fullness of Christian encounter. All sorts of potentialities open up. He finds within himself unexpected reserves of courage and compassion. Self-centeredness yields to interest in others, and the boundaries of his life are pushed outward. His relationships with God and others deepen and are enriched through love, freely given and received. Prayer becomes less a duty and more a source of strength. He no longer sees suffering in negative terms, but as a vehicle of growth. He is beginning to comprehend what St. Paul meant when he said, ". . . the life I live now is not my own; Christ is living in me." He is learning from experience the truth of Jesus' words: ". . . whoever loses his life for my sake will find it."

Stage 10
For Dave—as for all of us—evolution finally and completely comes about with the second coming of Christ, the resurrection of the body, the transformation of the universe into heaven, the break-out from the prison of time. Now life *really* begins. All the astounding promises of Christ come true. There is a new heaven and a new earth; God himself dwells with his people, and wipes away every tear from their eyes.

Those are the ten stages of the trip you may take if you turn on to God. When you read them, however, remember a few words of caution:

Remember that God works in many different ways and can draw many pictures.

Don't think of the journey as a rigid, mechanical process.

No one goes through the ten steps just by reading. The mere fact that you've *read* through them doesn't mean that you've *gone* through them.

Beware of playing the spiritual weightlifter. This is the person who thinks: "I'm moving up the list all by myself; I don't need anyone. Every day in every way, I'm getting better and better." This person forgets that we are dealing with encounters. It takes two to tango, two to form a friendship, two to marry, two to encounter.

Don't use the list to compare yourself to others. You might think you're doing better, and become a hypocrite. The Church has had enough trouble throughout the ages without creating more of them.

The list is not a Monopoly board (move forward seven spaces, pass GO, collect $200). It is offered to the person starting at zero, to give that person an overview, a glimpse of the big picture.

*   *   *   *   *

Remember that we've talked briefly about people who were baptized as infants and grew up in the Church without ever thinking much about how they got there or where they were going? These people are trying to go through Stages 7, 8, and 9 without ever having gone through steps 1 to 6. Like Bill, many of them are having second thoughts about the whole trip. Is there any way you can turn the plane around and start over so you can make up your own mind, like Joan? We think there is. We think we can guide you through Stages 1 to 6.

Okay. How do Stages 1 to 6 happen?

Before we begin to answer that one, we must make clear some basic rules. If, in the course of this journey, you become convinced that God is real and important, you will want to *relate* to him. Otherwise, the whole thing is just a head trip that takes you nowhere.

How do relationships work? They are two-way streets. The authors of this book wrote it in the conviction that God is real and important and already relating to you in love and care. But this may not be evident to you; in fact, it is the very obscurity and doubtful existence of God that may have motivated you to read this far.

Take, for example, the relationship between a parent and newly-born Karen. As an infant, Karen doesn't really love her parents. If she thinks at all, it is about herself. As far as she is concerned, the rest of the universe exists just to make her happy. But her mother and father love her intensely from the beginning. The fact that they receive no love in return does not discourage them. They know that gradually she will get to know them, and in knowing them return their love. So what starts out as a one-way relationship gradually becomes a two-way one. It only becomes a full love relationship when it is mutual or reciprocal.

The same may be said for the relationship between Karen and God. God from the beginning feels very strongly about her. She most likely doesn't reciprocate or return this love at first. In fact, she may not even think about God at all. She couldn't care less. She may not know God or even care to know him. And you can't love something you don't know. But God isn't discouraged. He freely loves her even though the relationship is just one-way. He hopes that gradually she will get to know him, and in doing so gradually get to love him. It's only when this relationship becomes two-way, when there is a giving-receiving on both sides, that things start happening and life becomes interesting.

A fellow and a girl generally do not fall in love with each other at exactly the same instant. One or the other has this love in the beginning and manifests it to the other. The hope is, of course, that in time the other one will return the love. Like a relationship with God, it is only then that love really blossoms out.

The same could be said for the relationship between any two friends. Once the friendship is two-way, things start to happen; we stop spinning our wheels; the action really starts.

One last preliminary word.

Before you can set out on this journey, you must become convinced of one thing: you are free. How far you go, where you stop, whether you go at all—is your decision.

Basically, religion is encounter—with God and with others. There can be no true encounter unless it is based on love. And it can't be love unless it's free.

If you fear that you are going to be manipulated, nothing is going to happen. That's why we, as authors, are absolutely obliged to respect your freedom. It's as simple as that. If we don't respect your freedom, we are undoing the very thing we hope will happen.

There seem to be a lot of people around who feel they have been manipulated in matters of religion. Whether in actual fact they have been is another matter. The important point is that they *feel* they've been manipulated. This is why we'd like to go back and start the journey over.

If, however, religion is encounter, then the person starting from zero has to do more than just read. If there is no meeting along the way, this book will be a waste of time. So, even while we scrupulously respect your freedom, we urge you from the beginning to try to go out of yourself and open up to the experience of encounter.

You know that in some societies marriages are made with the help of a matchmaker. The matchmaker can bring the couple together, can tell each of them how wonderful the other is. But no matchmaker can make them fall in love. That's up to them. In the same way, we can introduce you to God and to other people, but what happens next is up to you and them. Unless each freely decides to encounter the other, nothing is going to happen. Unless you choose God and God chooses you, no action. Unless you choose the other person and the other chooses you, pfffft. All we can do, like any matchmaker, is bring you together and hope for the best.

* * * * *

The first practical, concrete thing you can do is start a journal. This is your own private record of your thoughts, feelings, and experiences on this journey. It is meant for your eyes only, so writing style isn't important. All that matters is that you level with yourself and tell it like it is.

Sometimes you may share some of your journal reflections with the teacher or the group. This is completely up to you. Some things we like to share, some we prefer to keep to ourselves. That's as it should be.

Besides keeping the journal, you will engage in discussions and other activities indicated at the end of each chapter.

You take it from here.

Things to do

1. In your own words, explain how the stories of Bill and Joan relate to people's experience of religion and Church.
2. Many young and not-so-young people brought up in the Catholic Church are reexamining their faith and reconsidering their loyalties. Does this necessarily mean that in their case

something went wrong? Explain.
3. What does it mean to start the journey over, to start from zero? Do you think you could? Do you want to?
4. In reading the description of the Ten Stages, did you see yourself, or part of yourself, described in any of those stages?
5. Give an example of a one-way relationship in your life. Give an example of a two-way relationship in your life.
6. As you begin this journey, how do you feel? Where are you on this scale? Explain.

WHERE ARE YOU ON THIS SCALE?

ANGRY   HOSTILE   FEARFUL   CONFUSED   OPEN   OPTIMISTIC

CHAPTER 2

Don't Just Sit There

GOD IS A LITTLE RED-HEADED GIRL

All living is meeting.
— Martin Buber

The reader never sees some of the most important characters in the *Peanuts* comic strip. One of these is the little red-headed girl in Charlie Brown's school. For years he has been trying to get up courage to cross the school yard and introduce himself, but we know—and he knows—he never will. The problem is not with the girl, of course, but with Charlie. Full of hang-ups, burdened with a rotten self-image, he can't take the initiative in an encounter with another human being. It's too bad. You get the feeling that if he could just break the ice, the two of them might become good friends. Charlie keeps hoping that it will happen to him in spite of his doing nothing. Afraid to risk rejection and failure, he takes refuge in daydreams.

Did you ever return, after a few years, to your grammar-school yard? Did you notice how small it had become? The yard that looks so big to Charlie Brown is really very small. The distance and the difficulty are all in his own mind. So is the distance between us and others, between us and God.

The Japanese have an interesting word for encounter: *deai*. Actually, it's two words put together. *De* means *to go out of,* and *ai* means *to meet*. A very perceptive word. You must *go out* before you can *meet*. In fact, you must go out of yourself to meet the other, whether that other is God or another human being. There is a leap involved here—a leap out of yourself and toward the other —and it is scary. So scary that some people spend their lives avoiding the risk. They have associates, colleagues, acquaintances —but no friends. And others become experts on religion— scripture scholars, sociologists or psychologists of religion, even theologians—but have no faith. For them, the problem of relation-ships or of religion is just that: a problem, a puzzle, a head trip. And they get no closer to other people or to God than Charlie Brown gets to the red-headed girl.

Most people divide their life into compartments: work, play, sleep, travel. Each has its assigned percentage of life. If religion gets a share, it's usually just a few percent and assigned to the ornament class—nice to have, but not essential. Religion is handy at weddings and funerals, but I'm not going to lose any sleep over it.

Look at your life: work, play, sleep, travel. Every day is made up of experiences—good experiences, bad experiences, neutral experiences, boring experiences, hopeful experiences. As you try to locate yourself in these experiences, you find that they are bigger than you. You can't explain them solely in terms of your-self. You can't express what life is all about unless you go beyond yourself. You can't find the *full* meaning of any experience or event in your life until you extend it to include both yourself and the other.

Consider your life up to now. Pick out the three or four greatest happinesses in your life. If you examine them carefully, you'll find that for the most part they involve other people. Any experience in your life takes on full meaning only when it's done with someone, or for someone, or is shared in some way with someone.

There's a meeting with the someone, with the other—other people, or God. If you want to use a fancy word, there's an encounter. This meeting or encounter with God and others is what we call religion. Religion, seen from this point of view, is the most natural, the most ordinary thing in the world.

If we see religion as encounter, then *life* and *religion* are one and the same.

All day long the opportunity to encounter presents itself. You find yourself with people and so there's a chance to encounter them. (Just because you're with people doesn't necessarily mean that you "meet" or encounter them, but the opportunity is there.) There's nothing in your life that God isn't interested in. Not just the dramatic things, but also the humdrum things he finds interest-ing. He even finds you interesting. Suddenly life and religion are one.

As long as you see Christianity only as a system, an ethic, a philosophy—something to be studied the way you study history or math—nothing important happens. You may learn a lot about religion, but you'll never have faith. You may even learn something *about* God, but you won't *know* God. Even after you get your doctorate in theology and publish your tenth book on religion, you'll be an outsider, like Charlie Brown. The law is the same for scholars and mechanics, senior citizens and teenagers. You must take the risk, go out of yourself, and encounter God and others.

There will be a place for study afterwards. When people fall in love, they want to know more and more about each other—where they come from, where they live, their work, their interests, tastes, and ideas. When God becomes real and important to us, we want to know what he's really like . . . and study can help. But that's later . . . after you cross the schoolyard and introduce yourself. Come on, Charlie Brown, don't be wishy-washy.

The language we use to describe religious experience sometimes obscures the reality. We use expressions like "She has a deep faith," "He's very religious," "He prays a lot," "She's devoted to the Church." Maybe you've read this far in hopes of finding out how some people can be religious and say prayers without feeling phoney. The language is misleading because it gives the impression that religious experience centers about some *thing* . . . that faith, or Church, or prayer, just happen to be some people's "thing." This is sometimes true. There are people who use religion this way. But authentic religious experience isn't like that. It's not about some*thing*, but about Someone. A human being is caught up with a Reality infinitely greater than himself or herself—a Reality that's present in a mysterious way, a Reality that's personal. No word is adequate to express this Reality, but we have to use some word, and in our culture and language the word is God.

Some people say that this God is not really personal; he's just some force, or feeling, some energy at the heart of the universe. Still others say he's just a name for the love between people or for the best instincts of humankind. But Christians insist that God is personal—that he knows us by name, cares for us, speaks to us, listens to us. For people who are into genuine Christianity, religion and prayer and faith and Church are not values in themselves, but have great value because they're ways of being in touch with God.

Religion, then, is the attempt to relate to a personal God, to know and love One who knows and loves me first. Faith is more than an optimistic way of looking at the world; it's an abiding trust in a God who is faithful. Prayer is dialogue with God—sometimes speaking with him, sometimes listening, sometimes doing nothing but being with him. And a church is ideally a community which shares a faith in God and strives for union with him.

As you can see, in all this we're simply describing a relationship between persons. It's a very special one, to be sure, because one of the terms of the relationship is God himself. But, special as this relationship is, it's still subject to the laws that govern all interpersonal relationships. So if you want to know how a person can relate to God, you must first reflect on how you relate to other human beings. Consider, in particular, the relation of friendship.

How do you get to be friends? It can happen a thousand different ways. Two students sit next to each other in class, and they hit it off. Teammates on a basketball squad find they have something in common besides picks and jumpshots and dunks. A fellow and a girl meet at a dance and find they enjoy each other's company. Sometimes people start out disliking each other, but some shared experience turns it around and makes them friends. Most of these friendships aren't very deep or permanent. They fail to survive the end of summer vacation, graduation, or a change in address. Others go much deeper and endure for many years, even for a lifetime. Some are formalized in marriage, where two become one and share their whole lives in bonds of closest intimacy.

All these friendships, the brief and the lasting, the shallow and the deep, follow certain observable patterns. They begin with encounter, and they are nourished by dialogue, by sharing, and even by total self-giving, or they dwindle and fade because those things are lacking.

Before you can become someone's friend, you must encounter that person. By this time you have already sat next to over a hundred kids in school. Some you got to know. About others, you never cared one way or the other. If you ever became pals with one, it was by sharing something—asking for help, enjoying a laugh together, working together on a project, maybe just being bored by the same teacher. You shared your feelings, your time, your opinions. You did things together after school and on weekends. When that happens, you have a friend—maybe even a close friend. The other kids sitting near you are just *there:* this one

is *with* you. When you need help, this person is the one you turn to, the first one you tell good news to. There are secrets you share with no one else. This is the stuff of friendship, and it starts when two people notice each other, let down their defenses, and begin to build a relationship.

That's how we meet our friends. And that's how we meet God, too. He's always there, waiting for us to notice and respond. He's always with us, even when we're not with him. But he won't force himself on us. As with any other potential friend, we must open ourselves up to him.

In other words, the first thing we must do is pray.

Now that may seem like an odd way to begin. How can we pray to someone when we're not even sure he exists? How can we pray until and unless we have faith? Aren't we putting the cart before the horse? Worse yet, isn't this a kind of manipulation, a psychological trick to get the religion monkey on my back?

Not really. Even if you're not sure you believe in God at this stage, you should try to pray. You must take that leap and go out of yourself, willing to share and to receive. There has to be *de* before there can be *ai*—a meeting, an encounter. Pray and see what happens.

Well, all right, I'll try it. But *how*?

1. Pray in your own words, if you want. Tell God what's in your heart and on your mind, right at this moment. Don't make your language too formal. It's hard to develop a friendship when people are stiff and formal with each other.

2. You don't have to use words at all, if you don't want to. Think *together with God* about your life. That's praying.

3. Imagine yourself on a hike with a friend. In the beginning it's "yak, yak, yak." As you go along, though, and begin to climb mountains, the words become fewer and fewer. Finally the two of your arrive out of breath at the top. A magnificent scene lies at your feet. No words are spoken. Who needs them? Encounter without words.

4. Try to be aware, if only for a moment, that God is with you. He's with you and finds you interesting. You can become aware of God anytime, anyplace—riding on a train, walking to school, having a coke, watching television, working at your job. In your awareness of God, these activities—the train ride, the walk, the work—can become prayer.

5. Open a Bible and read slowly and reflectively. Not all

parts of the Bible are appropriate, but many are. In the New Testament, the words and deeds of Christ can be thought-provoking and inspirational. This is the prayer of listening. In the Old Testament, the Psalms are prayers you can say yourself. These are poems and songs that people have used for over 2,500 years in meeting God. They express universal experiences and emotions like sadness, thanksgiving, loneliness, cries for help. You can find one to fit any mood or situation.

6. Take part in a Eucharist celebration. This last suggestion may not seem very attractive, especially if you've had bad experiences and have been turned off by the Mass. But try to take a fresh look. The first half of the Eucharist is a dialogue in which we talk to God in prayer together, and he talks to us through Scripture and preaching. The second half is an encounter in which we give of self to God, and he gives himself to us. (Somehow, too, we meet the others at the Eucharist in a deeper way than just being in the same room together.)

These are just some of the ways you might try to pray. Choose ways you feel comfortable with. Prayer may come much more easily than you think. And even if it doesn't . . . if you find stubborn resistance or inertia within yourself . . . or if you feel that you're speaking into a void . . . don't give up too easily. Some of the most valuable things in our lives don't come easily at first. This may be a good time to find out if you're serious.

Things to do

1. What is the point of the Charlie Brown story? What does it have to do with religion?
2. The basic theme of this chapter can be expressed in the following equation: Religion = Encounter = Life
   Explain this in your own words.
3. "Religion is not about some*thing* but about Someone." Explain.
4. What is the difference between knowing about God and knowing God?
5. From your own life, give the case history of a friendship. How did it start? How did it develop? Is it still going on, or is it a thing of the past? What made these things happen?
6. Make one or more suggested attempts at prayer. Write in your journal how it went. Feel free to share all or part or none of it with the others in the group.

CHAPTER 3

We're Moving!

THE BEST IS YET TO COME

When we try to relate to God and other people and open ourselves to encounter with them, we win a few and lose a few. We don't always understand why we have these ups and downs. What did I do right? Where did I go wrong? In the face of failure, why bother?

When we start asking questions like these, whether we know it or not, we're reflecting on the dynamics of encountering God and others. And if we're really going to understand them, we must first do something even more basic: we must understand ourselves.

You have to understand the You.

But you really can't understand the You except against a cosmic backdrop. You must situate yourself in the Big Picture. Where do you fit in the larger scheme of things?

To find the answer, you must understand what the big picture is, what constitutes the larger scheme of things, the game plan of the universe.

It's Evolution.

The whole universe has been, and still is, in movement. It's engaged in a dynamic process of growth and development, and you and I are part of it. We're all in this together.

The fact that the universe doesn't *seem* to be evolving means nothing. A baby riding on a train thinks the world of people, seats, and walls is motionless. Then the child looks out the window . . . we're moving!! An adult, too, can sit in a jet plane and feel motionless when he or she is actually moving at 600 miles an hour.

You can't understand your world or your place in it until you recognize that you're moving, and the whole world with you. But where have we come from, and where are we going? And who's in charge?

To begin to answer these questions, let's recall a certain television show and then imagine a movie they'll never make.

Did you ever see that TV spot that showed the history of the United States in two minutes? Two hundred years flashed by in 120 seconds, as pictures of famous Americans and historic events succeeded one another at lightning speed. It was almost too much too fast to take in, but it worked, and the viewer caught the sweep of events in our country's first two centuries.

Now suppose we tried to make a two-hour film of the history of our evolving universe. Recall the key events that will flash before us on the screen: first the "big bang," the cosmic explosion that probably gave birth to our world, including the stars and planets. Then on our earth we watch the oceans gradually produce the first organisms, the beginning of life. Later, these organisms appear on land and move up the evolutionary ladder to mammals and, "finally," to us humans.

If we try to keep the film in proportion, and give each evolutionary phase its proper allotment of time, we come up with some astounding results. Among scientists, the best current estimate of the age of the universe is about 15 billion years. The first appearance of humans is usually placed about two million years ago. Two million seems like a lot. But in that two-hour film, do you know when humans appear? In the last *two seconds*.

Of course, the film isn't over yet. But it's obvious that, in a manner of speaking, we humans have just arrived. And if you really look at the big picture, you realize what that makes us. Primitives. True, we dropped leopard skins a while back, but we've just started. The best is yet to come.

Look at it another way. Represent the world and its history by the Washington Monument. In those 555 feet, the whole story of the human race covers about one quarter of an inch. The thickness of several coats of paint.

If such considerations make us feel tiny and insignificant, we miss the point. What matters is that the show isn't over. The most exciting and important part has just begun, and we're part of it. The rest of the script hasn't yet been written. Who's going to write it? WHO ELSE? You. Me. We're moving! Where do you want to go?

As soon as you put the question that way, you're on the right track. You've stopped thinking like a person in a static world. You've looked out the train window and realized you're moving. You perceive the world in an evolutionary framework, and you've begun to think like the evolving being you are.

So what? So plenty.

In a static universe, the most important thing is to preserve, and the worst thing is to make a mistake.

In an evolving universe, the most important thing is to search, and the worst thing is not to try.

* * * * *

As we look at this big picture, this overview of all the action, three themes emerge that you can apply to your life:

1) We advance by falling down and getting up.
2) What looks like a winner isn't always a winner.
3) When things get together, things happen.

First Principle:
We advance by falling down and getting up.
God is quite an artist. He's been working on his masterpiece, the universe, for billions of years, and it seems he still has a long way to go. We tend to think that God just wound up the universe like a clock, put it down, and went away. No way. He's busy day and night, here, there, and everywhere. You've never seen such a busy artist.

As God works on his masterpiece and the universe evolves, we notice that the world (the human race included) advances by falling on its face. Looking at any aspect of evolution, we see many probings, many failures, many flops, many blind alleys. From time to time there's a breakthrough, and success.

Evolution works this way for individuals, too. It is not mistakes or failures that keep a person from growing, but the refusal to try, to take chances.

Pee Wee Reese was a great shortstop when he played for the old Brooklyn Dodgers in the '40s and '50s. He made more errors than many of his competitors, but he was generally acknowledged as the best at his position because he covered more territory and fielded more grounders than they did. Students of the game knew that what mattered wasn't the occasional fumble, but the grounders he reached and turned into outs when no one else could. On the other hand, Zeke Bonura, a hard-hitting, colorful first baseman with the White Sox and Giants, was so inept in the field (at least by big-league standards), that fans used to argue whether he let in more runs for the other team than he drove in for his own. Yet Bonura's fielding average was usually near the top of the league, for he made few actual errors. The knock on Zeke was that he just waved at too many grounders as they went by. It wasn't what he did *wrong* that hurt; it was what he didn't try to do *right*.

Well, baseball is a difficult game, and we shouldn't be too hard on Mr. Bonura. But when you think of it, that's Charlie Brown's problem, too. He's afraid of being turned down by the little red-headed girl. Let's re-word the old chestnut a bit: ''Better to have tried and failed than never to have tried at all.''

Second Principle:

What looks like a winner isn't always a winner.

Whatever happened to the dinosaur, anyway? Talk about big losers! How is it that it disappeared?

Denis the Dinosaur certainly looked like a winner as he stomped around, while all the other, smaller animals ran for cover. But appearances were deceiving. It was the much smaller mammal, cowering in a cave at the dinosaur's approach, that was really at the center of the action.

Conrad the Caveman didn't look like a winner. The other animals in the neighborhood could run faster, climb higher, and score better in paw-to-paw combat. But good old Conrad, with his skimpy fur, harmless teeth, and funny bow-legged gait, was at the central thrust of evolution. He didn't just survive. He even got to run the show.

A few billion years ago, which would have seemed more durable—a giant rock, or some microscopic algae? Yet the rocks have worn away under the ceaseless erosion of time, while the algae gave birth to ever more complex forms of life, climaxing in the genesis of humans.

Even today, an extraterrestrial visitor, seeing our solar system for the first time, would find the planet Jupiter much more impressive than Earth. It's 1,400 times as big, and its gravitational pull many times greater. But cheer up, earthlings! Compared to our scene, Jupiter is a loser: no life, no intelligence. As somebody said about Oakland, there's no *there* there. To W.C. Fields, Jupiter would have made even Philadelphia look good.

How about that carpenter up in the Galilean hills 1,950 years ago? Making chairs and tables for obscure people in a hick town in a politically third-rate country . . . . If that isn't Dullsville, what is? Compare him with the governor of a Roman province, administering vast territories and populations and being responsible directly to the Emperor. No comparison, huh? True, but not the way

you would have expected. The big shot has been forgotten (and deservedly so) by all but a few students of ancient history. The carpenter, who looked like a nowhere man, was right at the center of evolution's thrust.

How about you? You may not look like a winner. You may not be famous. Your picture isn't in the newspaper every day. Even in the small world of your own school, you may not be a V.I.P. And yet you may be right where the action is; you may be right at the central thrust of evolution.

To see how, you must grasp our third principle.

Third Principle:
When things get together, things happen.
As we look at the history of the universe, we see a very interesting situation arise time and time again. When things get together, things happen. Atoms get together, and order emerges from chaos. Molecules get together, and we begin to get life. Humans come out of their caves and get together with other humans, and we begin to get civilization. Dispersed things get together, and there is progress. And get this: not only is there progress, but there is a breakthrough, a dramatic leap forward.

What's the message for you personally? It's this: You can't evolve, you can't blossom out into the interesting person you're meant to be, all by your lonesome. You must get together—with God and with other people—for things to happen. But this can't happen unless you want it to. Although the human race and the world as a whole is inevitably going to evolve, you as an individual may or may not. How come? Because you're free. No one can make you evolve if you don't want to.

Free will is one of the most marvelous things about a person. If a puppy dog comes up to you wagging his tail and nuzzling your hand, it's nice. But you know that if your lap goes away, he'll quickly go and find another one. For you realize he came to you not by choice but by instinct.

If, on the other hand, a human being comes to you and says, with or without words, ''Hey, I want to be your friend!'' or, ''I love you!''—this really turns you on. Why? Because this person freely chose you . . . went out of his or her way to pick you. Wow! And you are free to respond, or to hold back; to take a chance on growth, or to play it safe and stay right where you are.

Because you're free, you can choose to evolve along with the rest of the universe, or to hold back and let the world pass you by.

To evolve, what must you do? If you've reached the point where you can ask that question, and really want an answer, then it's time to stop talking and to act.

Here are three things to do. The first two you should do right now, before you read or discuss any more. The third one will take longer, but now's the time to start.

Project One:
Do a review of your life up till now.
This isn't an examination of conscience. In an examination of conscience you're interested in what you did right or what you did wrong. What we're after here is a review of your whole life. What do you think of it up to now? There are some things you had no control over: where you were born, how tall you are, whether you have a good singing voice. There are many other elements over which you did have control.

Okay, what we want is a general review of the whole thing. Don't be too strict or too easy. Don't be too optimistic or too pessimistic. Strive for reality. You're not going to type this out and hand it to anyone; it's just for yourself.

If you find it hard to get started, here are some suggested points to cover:

— *People* in my life. Who played the leading roles? How? Did I play a part in others' lives?

—*Things* I've done. Accomplishments. Disappointments. High points? Low points?

—*Places* I've been. Where I've lived. Where I just touched base or passed through. Did they make a difference?

—*Turning points.* Any pivotal events that set or changed the direction of my life. Or has it been pretty much a straight line?

—*Goals*, *values*, *hopes*, *fears*, *hang-ups*, *ideals*. What are the things that have moved me . . . or stopped me . . . or turned me aside? What have I been seeking . . . or running from? What has made me tick?

Project Two:
Spell out what you want to happen in life.
Here we want you to really pull the stops out, blow your mind, let loose. Tell yourself what you really want to happen in your life.

Actually, most of us are small-time operators. We're afraid to think big. We brag about how nothing or no one is going to fence us in, and then we spend most of our time fencing ourselves in.

Many young people have a tunnel vision of their future. They talk a great game of freedom, but they actually have a very limited and narrow view of what they want out of their existence. What they want from life is mostly just what they can attain by themselves. So their future is mostly a tunnel they walk alone.

In this state of mind, they're not open to most religious messages.

Now if, by Personal Evolution Action, they expand their heart wishes—what they want out of their future existence—what happens?

They realize they cannot attain these expanded heart wishes by themselves. They realize they need God and others. They see they have to encounter God and others. This, by the way, is our working description of religion: Religion = Encountering God and Others.

So think big . . . . Let yourself go. Take off like a rocket. Don't be afraid to dream! What do you want to happen from here on in?

Project Three:
Start to make it happen.
As you did Project Two, you may have noticed certain basic desires emerge. If they did, it's because God put them in your heart. Among them are probably these:
—You want to love.
—You want to be loved.
—You want to encounter, to share with the other.
—You want to blossom out . . . to realize all your potentialities and abilities to the full.

Concretely, how you want these things to happen may differ from what the next person wants. But when you let yourself dream big, these desires are going to appear.

Now it's time to get down to business, to start *doing* things to make those desires happen, to make those dreams come true. And you can do it, if you avoid falling into either of two traps.

The first trap is to become a dynamic non-doer. The dynamic non-doer is long on talk, tops on theory, great on plans and dreams—but short on action, short on real openness and real ability to change and do.

(Just an aside. Occasionally, you will meet a person who's really marvelous at Project Two. We don't mean this sarcastically. This person is not a pipe dreamer. In fact, this person has wonderful aspirations, really cares for others, honestly wants to do some great things, and has a tremendous capacity for love. When it comes to doing something to bring all this about, and the action is ordinary—fine, no problem. But if it involves a real sacrifice, a real change, a real "leap" to the other—then nothing happens.)

The other trap you can fall into is to become a hundred-percenter. If the hundred-percenter can't attain 100 percent of all the desires uncovered in Project Two, then he or she wants out. Such people want no part of life; they want to cop out. If they can't excel with 100 percent, then they're going to excel with zero percent . The name of the game, ladies and gentlemen, is that you may not attain 100 percent in this phase of your life. (The batter who hits .333 is put out twice as often as he hits safely.) You may have to settle for less than 100 percent in this phase of your life. Maybe far less.

Well, then, why did we urge you to blow your mind and dream big? Were we putting you on? Nope. You must understand that it's God who's in charge of evolution. He put those basic aspirations and desires in your heart. And he's going to fulfill them. He's going to fulfill them a million times over when evolution finally and completely comes about at the resurrection of your body, at Christ's second coming, when the universe becomes heaven, and we blow the prison of time, and life really begins!

Project Four:
Get together with God and others.
But you're not going to evolve all by yourself. We saw a short time ago that things happen when things get together. That applies to you—in spades. You're not going to evolve until you get together with God and with other people. Which is nothing more or less than our definition of religion.

* * * * *

So we're turning you loose. From now on, as we move together through this book, we hope you'll be *doing* as well as *reading.* But in turning you loose, we're not going to leave you alone without help. In the next chapter, we'll begin to examine what happens when you encounter God and encounter others in a love situation.

Things to do
1. What does evolution have to do with all this?
2. Take the three themes of evolution and show how they're verified or exemplified in your own life or in the lives of people you know.
3. Do Project One and Project Two. Put them in your journal. You may keep them to yourself or share some or all of them with the group.
4. As you can see, Project Three is going to be a big part of this whole journey. Do you see this as something to start now or have you already begun in some way?

CHAPTER 4

Going My Way?

MEETING GOD AND OTHERS

When we get together, either with God or with others, we're in a love situation. A few chapters earlier, in trying to describe this process of getting together, we used the Japanese word *dei*. It means *to go out* and then *to meet*—to encounter. Everyone wants to love and be loved, but love can't happen unless there's an encounter. There must be a leap out of oneself. And it's scary.

We all have a lot of acquaintances but not too many friends. It's easy to become an acquaintance; it's tough to become a friend. Becoming an acquaintance is like moving over some flat land. Becoming a friend is like jumping over a deep ditch to someone on the other side.

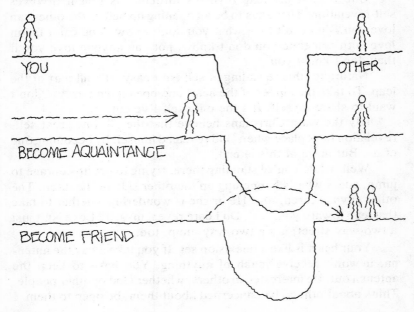

YOU

OTHER

BECOME AQUAINTANCE

BECOME FRIEND

That leap is scary. One push from the other and down we go into the ditch. We leap; the other refuses to accept us, and down we tumble.

It's not too hard to shake hands with someone. Even though you extend your right hand, you can still protect yourself with your other hand. Most likely, the first two people who shook hands didn't trust each other very much. They were probably holding out their right hands to show they weren't going for their swords. (Now if one of them was left-handed . . . .)

If you go to embrace someone, it's a different story. You're wide open. No defense. If the other decides to let you have it, you've had it.

There appears to be a law of life that goes like this:

Beyond the difficulty

Beyond the adventure

Beyond the leap

Is

Joy.

There's no denying the difficulty and the adventure in leaping from oneself to the other. There is no denying the joy in encountering the other.

One reason the leap involves difficulty is that it involves self-revelation. There has to be an opening up before the other can love you. You can't love what you don't know. You can't fall in love with someone you don't know, nor can anyone love you if they don't know you.

Naturally, this revealing of self isn't easy. It's all part of the leap. To take the zipper of the heart and open it isn't easy. I don't want to share myself. It's the only self I've got.

(By the way, Christians believe that the all-time great self-revelation took place when God revealed himself by becoming one of us. But more of this later.)

Well, while you're standing there, trying to get up courage to jump, guess what's happening on the other side of the ditch. The other guy is scared, too! He or she is wondering whether to take that leap toward you . . . . Do I dare reveal myself? Love isn't just a two-way street; it's a two-way jump, too.

Your heart is like a television set. If you take away the antenna, it won't receive much of anything. You have to keep the antenna out. Be interested in others, whether God or other people. Think about others, be concerned about them, be open to them. I wonder if that person is happy or sad. I'd like to get to know that person.

Not too many people are going to come up to you and say, "Hey, I'd like to love you" or "Hey, I'd like to be your friend." We're generally a bit uptight about things like that. People are usually more indirect. They send out some hints, some signals. That's why you have to keep the antenna out.

Keep the antenna out for God, too. It's been years since he used the thunder-and-lightning routine. Why? Well, if he zaps you, where's your freedom? And what kind of encounter is it if it's not free? God doesn't want to put a gun to your head and kidnap you. His voice is usually not thunder and lightning, but a smaller one in your heart.

> Elijah came to a cave, where he took shelter. Then the Lord said, "Go outside and stand on the mountain before the Lord; the Lord will be passing by." A strong and heavy wind was rending the mountains and crushing rocks before the Lord—but the Lord was not in the wind. After the wind there was an earthquake—but the Lord was not in the earthquake. After the earthquake there was fire—but the Lord was not in the fire. After the fire there was a tiny whispering sound. When he heard this, Elijah hid his face in his cloak and went and stood at the entrance of the cave.
>
> —1 Kings 19:9,11-13

But it's frightening, going out like this and leaving myself wide open. Why not stay in the cave where it's safe? Suppose I don't leap that ditch? What's to lose? What's to gain?

The best way to answer that one is to imagine myself getting shipwrecked. There I am on a comfortably warm desert island with plenty of supplies, a stocked freezer, and my own coke machine. Not bad at first. The peace and quiet are beautiful. But after a while, even if there are no problems with food, clothing, or shelter, I start to go up the walls. Man, am I lonely!

Did you ever wonder why we can get lonely? Now you take God . . . God never gets lonely. Why? Because in God's inner life there is an I and a You. The I is constantly meeting with the You; the You is constantly encountering the I. The I is interested in and loves the You; the You is interested in and loves the I. The I and the You share all with each other. Call the I, Father. Call the You,

Son. This meeting, this love between the Father and the Son is so intense, so vivid, so strong, so alive, that it's a Person, called the Holy Spirit.

God made us like himself, but with an important difference. Within me is just the "I." The "you" is outside. The I within me is always going to seek the you . . . to want to love and to be loved by the you. The "you" is the other; it's God, it's fellow humans. If I really know myself, then I know that this is more basic to me than my own heartbeat—to seek the "you."

Well, then, suppose I build a boat and leave my tight little island. Imagine that I've left the cave . . . jumped the ditch. What will I find? Love?

We thought you'd never ask.

What is love, anyway? Don't ask for a 100 percent definition, because you're not going to get it. Love is too close, too intimate. It's easy to see other people's faces in a room, but very hard to see your own. It's too close. The same with love.

We can't define it, but we can describe it.

A young fellow and a girl on a date are walking down the street. Out of the bushes jumps your friendly TV reporter, microphone ready for an interview. "Why," he asks each in turn, "do you date this person?"

Their answers are basically the same: When we go out with each other, it feels great. It's nice to be together, so we date.

Tom and Jenny may not yet be in love. If you stop and analyze it, our two friends are really interested in each other for their own feelings. Tom dates Jenny because it makes him feel good. Jenny dates Tom because it makes a nice evening for her. Of course, there's nothing wrong with this. We're not criticizing. But let's say that at this stage they're just in the doorway to love.

Time passes. Six months later. Same fellow, same girl, same friendly TV reporter, same question. Their answers are somewhat the same, but with some revealing differences.

Jenny (and later Tom) responds: "Why do I like to be with Tom? I like to make him happy, and I try to. When I see Tom happy, I'm happy too. I rejoice in his happiness. When he's sad, I try to help him, to end the sorrow. If there's nothing I can do (Tom may be sick, and I'm not a doctor), at least I can share his sorrow.

"I like to share not only the extremes of joy and sorrow, but also the ordinary things in his life. Doing something with Tom, even if it's humdrum, is interesting. I'm interested in his opinions.

I may not always agree with them, but I'm interested in them.

"And this is the most amazing part of all. Tom likes to be with me, to make me happy. When I'm happy, he rejoices. When I'm sad, he tries to help. If he can't do anything, at least he'll go half-and-half with my sorrow.

"Not only joy and sorrow, but the ordinary things in my life interest him. He wants to share even the humdrum things in my life. When he shares them, they're not so boring any more. He may not always buy my opinions, but at least he's interested in them. Joy, sorrow, ordinary stuff, you name it, and there's Tom."

Now we're on the trail of love. What we have here is a dynamic giving-receiving. There's that forgetting of self, that leap toward the other, that giving of self, that self-revelation, that desire to make the other happy. And lo and behold, the other thinks of me, leaps toward me, reveals and gives of self to me, and wants to make me happy! It bears a remarkable resemblance to the mutual giving and receiving that take place in the inner life of God.

What is love? We can say three things about it:
1. Love is a triangle.
2. Love is being able to say, "I know how you feel."
3. Love is a campfire.

1. *Love is a triangle.*
God is at one corner, you at another, and other people at the third.

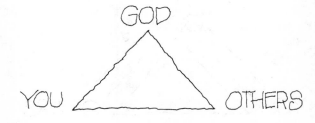

The first thing that happens is that God loves you, and he loves other people.

He starts things rolling: he makes the first leap. In the beginning we don't love God. One reason is, we may not know him. How can you love someone you don't know? But he doesn't get discouraged any more than the parent of a newly-born child gets discouraged. The parent loves the child right from the start. But it's a one-way street. All the baby wants is to be fed, burped, and changed. The child doesn't love the parent, but the parent is in no hurry. For gradually the child will get to know the parent, and in knowing, begin to love in return. What starts out as a one-way street gradually becomes a two-way love relationship.

The same with God. He's not discouraged: he keeps loving. His hope is that, in time, you (and others) will get to know him, and in doing so come to love him. What starts out as a one-way street will gradually become a mutual love relationship.

It's God who brings us together in this life. Thanks to God, you have many wonderful meetings with other people in your life.

It's because of the love you receive from God that you have the ability to love others. It's because of the love others receive from God that they have the ability to love you.

In the beginning you may not love God, you may not know God, you may not advert to God, and yet you go around loving other people. What gives? You may never advert to God, yet he's loving you every day, and it's thanks to that love that you're able to love others.

You may step into a room, turn on the light switch, and never advert to the generator that's producing the electricity. It's thanks to the generator, however, that the light goes on. Of course, what we're dealing with here is not some generator in the sky, but a loving personal God. And so, thanks to God, we love each other.

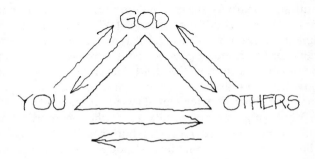

Just one little extra point. You can't love without being loved. If you cut yourself off from receiving love, you may still be able to love for a short time, but you're going to dry up very soon.

2. *Love is being able to say, "I know how you feel."*
Imagine that you're going to Japan—not as a tourist, but to live there with the people for five years.

When you go to Japan this way, you die and have to be born again. You leave America as a relatively educated person and enter Japan as a dummy, an idiot, a barbarian.

You don't know how to eat (chopsticks); even if you do, you're not too sure you want to (today's special, raw fish). You don't know how to sit (on your ankles on the floor, it hurts). You don't know how to go into a house (take your shoes off, dummy). You don't know how to take a bath (wash before you get into the boiling water, you idiot). If you want to go shopping, someone has to take you, because with your lack of Japanese you could easily get lost. You're a barbarian specializing in social blunders from morning to night.

Because the Japanese language is so complicated, you find yourself in a strange situation. It's as though you were standing in a hallway, with a series of closed doors on your left and right. The doors are labeled: expression of past experiences, expression of present emotions, expression about history, expression about literature, expression about life, expression about love. Now on each door there are two locks. One has been opened by training and experiences in America. The other can be opened only by knowing the Japanese language. And, as yet, you can't open it. So you stand humiliated, alone and lonely, in the hallway.

Gradually, of course, you begin to learn the language (which you continue to learn for the rest of your life). But it's complicated. Ordinarily, the subject of the sentence (Who did it?) isn't expressed. Singular or plural isn't expressed (the same word is used for one friend or ten friends). Gender isn't expressed (someone can talk to you about a third person for ten minutes and you still may not know if it's a man or a woman). And so it goes.

So what happens? After a lot of sweat you can talk about many things. You can go shopping, talk about the weather, take a trip without getting lost, order in a restaurant. That's progress, all right, but a big problem remains. Although you're functioning in the language, it's still so complicated it may take you up to four years before you can have a heart-to-heart talk with anyone. Now this is a heavy cross, because you're a people person. There's so much you want to say! There's so much you want to hear! It's as though you were in an isolation booth surrounded by people—and dying of loneliness.

When you go to Japan, you die, and have to be born again.

And then when another newcomer arrives, and says, "I'm confused," you can say, "I know how you feel." He or she may confide in you and tell you, "This whole bit is new, confusing, scary." And you know what he or she is talking about—not just in your head, but in your guts. The person tells you, "I'm lonely." You say, "I know what you're talking about." You can share the other's feelings the way no one else can who hasn't actually experienced them.

Now, you don't have to go to Japan to share an emotion with someone. You can do it anywhere, with any one, in any situation. Here's how:

i. *Recall your own experience*. It doesn't have to be identical with the other's experience, just similar . . . a sorrow, a hurt, a confusion, a loneliness.

ii. *Feel with the other*. This is what the word *sympathy* meant originally—not to *feel sorry for*, but *to feel with* the other. I may feel sorry for that poor guy who got hit by a car, but if I've never been in an accident, it doesn't have much to do with me.

iii. *Share the experience/feeling with the other*. The other, in some way, can give you a part of it. He or she is no longer alone.

Here are some other points to keep in mind:

—The experience/emotion doesn't have to be a difficult one. It can be a joy, a happiness, a surprise, a hope.

—You can be the one with the experience/emotion. And someone can share it with you.

—What if God entered into the human condition? Could he not then share with you? Would he know how we feel?

3. *Love is like a campfire*.

Love is not like a pie; it's like a campfire. Most people think love is like a pie, with just so many slices. There's a slice for God, a slice for husband or wife, a few slices for the kids, and a few slices for others.

"Sorry, God, but if I give you a bigger slice, there just won't be enough to go around. Sorry, wife or husband, but you know how it is. If I give you a bigger slice, everyone else goes short. What are you yelling about, kids? You're getting your slices, aren't you? (Sorry, Mom and Dad, I'm giving the whole pie to my latest boyfriend!) Sorry, all you people out there, but aside from a few of you, there are no more slices to go around!"

The source of love—any love—is God. He's infinite, without any limits, while we're limited. But our capacity to love and to be loved can grow. That's why it's like a campfire.

To start a campfire, you begin small, with a few twigs. Once you get these lit, you put on some wood that's a little bigger. And once that catches fire and is burning nicely, you add bigger and bigger wood, until you're using logs. Now you have a real campfire going; and if you feel like it, you can build it up into a bonfire.

Inside you there's a fire waiting to be lit. The more you love, the greater is your capacity to love. The more you love God, the more you're able to love people around you. And the more you love them, the more you're able to love God. The more you love your wife or husband, the more you're able to love the kids. The more you love your kids, the more you're able to love your husband or wife. The more you love family, the more you can love others. The more you love others, the more you can love family.

That's the difference between pies and campfires. The more wood you throw on a campfire, the more wood it can absorb.

And it's nice to know that the more you're loved, the more you're capable of being loved.

* * * * *

One last word. Before any of these fires get lit, before we take any leaps toward others, there's one indispensable condition. You can't love other persons or God unless you love one person in particular. Can you guess who?

Who else but yourself?

God says you must love your neighbor as yourself. When we hear that, we usually start thinking about our neighbor—who that is and whether we can love him or her. We take that second part—"as yourself"—for granted. And why not? Don't all people love themselves too much?

Sometimes, but not very often. You might be surprised to know how many people don't like what they see in the mirror. We're not talking about faults and failings. It's natural to dislike our failings. We're talking about people who don't like *themselves*. They're really unhappy being in their own presence. They really don't love themselves.

If you don't like your face or your figure or your faults, that's okay. But if you don't love *yourself*, then you can't love God or others either. Why? Well, when you love somebody, what you're doing is giving yourself as a gift to that person. If you don't love yourself, then you rate yourself as nothing, and you have nothing to give.

When you think of it, isn't that Charlie Brown's problem? The underlying reason why he'll never cross the schoolyard and say hello to the little red-headed girl is that he thinks he's a nothing. He can't relate because he thinks he has nothing to give.

If you do love yourself, then what you're saying when you love someone is: "Here, I give you myself. I'm not perfect. I'm not the greatest thing since canned beer. But I'm all I've got, and I give it to you."

Things to do
1. A genuine human encounter involves a leap and that leap is often scary. Why?
2. Have you ever made such a leap? Was it scary? Did you end up in the ditch or on the other side?
3. When we reveal ourselves and go out to others, we can be hurt. Isn't it safer to stay on our side of the ditch? What do we have to lose?
4. Love is being able to say, "I know how you feel." From a movie or a play or a novel or short story, find an example of this truth.
5. "Love isn't like a pie; it's like a campfire." What does this mean? Why is it important?
6. Why is it that some people don't love themselves?

CHAPTER 5

Getting To Know You

PEOPLE WHO NEED PEOPLE

If you're going to collect stamps, you should know something about stamps.

If you're going to grow flowers, you should know something about flowers.

If you're going to raise chipmunks, you should know something about chipmunks.

If you're going to encounter people, you should know something about people.

The more you know about people and the better you understand them, the better your chance of relating to them. What can we tell you about them when they're so different, and each individual is not quite the same as any other? Well, there are certain basic characteristics common to all persons. This chapter is about four of them. Being aware of these four characteristics, and paying attention to them, can help you understand people and relate to them. And don't forget—since *you* are a person, too, these characteristics apply to you as well.

Four things you should know about people are:
1. People are social.
2. People are mysterious.
3. People are influential.
4. People are interesting.

1. *People are social.*
Imagine that we've kidnapped a year-old baby girl, put her in a plane, and left her all alone on a deserted island in the Pacific.

The baby's chances of survival are very slim. She can't move around very well; she can't eat or drink by herself, she doesn't know how to provide food or shelter. Without others, she can't satisfy the most basic needs of existence. In fact, her existence in the first place is due to others.

Suppose, just suppose, this baby survives, and we meet her on our return to this island twenty years later. She's in sad shape. She knows no history, no literature; she doesn't even know how to talk. Worst of all, she knows no human encounter, no human relationships. She's never experienced giving or receiving from another human being. She knows no friendship. She's never heard of love.

This far-out example underlines a very important fact about human beings. They need many *things,* but they need other *people* most of all. For mere physical survival, *things* might be enough; but to exist as human beings, they need something more. And we don't have to go to desert islands to observe this. Some of the wealthiest, most envied people have been the most miserable, when they found they could buy everything except human love. Encounter and dialogue are the very stuff of life; human relationships aren't luxuries, they're the most basic necessities of existence.

2. *People are mysterious.*
Humans are like God, and so there's tremendous depth to them. They have infinite possibilities. They're a mystery.

We can study a wristwatch for five years, and by that time we know it inside out. But we could study you for five years, or ten or twenty, and we would have just scratched the surface. We'll never know you completely, because there's always more to the God-like you. That's why people are mysterious.

This also explains why it's easier to get angry at a person than at a wristwatch. When two people with infinite depth and unlimited possibilities get together, it's very easy for both of them, even with the best intentions, to relate on different levels. And then what happens? A misunderstanding.

It's easier to get angry at a person than at a wristwatch, but then again, it's easier to fall in love with a person than with a wristwatch.

3. *People are influential.*
A fascinating thing takes place in friendship. Everyone has some bad points, even (sob!) you. Now, what happens in friendship is

that the influence of your friend gradually causes your bad points to diminish. The love someone has for you, perhaps his or her good example and desire to make you happy, all help to whittle down and even remove some of your failings. Of course, you have the same effect on the other person.

Much more important than your bad points are your good points. And this mutual influence works here, too. The love your friend has for you, his or her good example and desire to make you happy—all help bring out your good points. Those interesting qualities that make up the Real You blossom out . . . and the same thing is happening to the other person. You're good for each other. Because of your friendship, each of you is a better person.

Don't doubt for a moment that those good points are far more important than the bad ones, for both of you. Many people think, wrongly, that a saint is a person with no minus signs. Far from it. A newborn baby has no minus signs, but neither has he or she any plus signs—which is why we call the baby innocent, but not a saint. A saint has minus signs, too; what makes a person a saint is that his or her plus signs are so fascinating.

God, of course, has a lot to do with people becoming saints. Even if you and your friend don't get that far, God is also helping you influence each other. Although God meets you directly, he also meets you through others. This is one of the central mysteries of life: God encounters people through people.

4. *People are interesting.*
Put a batch of photos on the table. Pictures of buildings, pictures of scenery, pictures of people . . . a couple hundred snapshots are spread out. Which will be picked up most often? Which ones will be looked at time and again? People photos, of course. People are interesting.

Unfortunately, many times we don't take an interest in people. And then we wonder why our life is boring.

Naturally, you should be thinking about yourself much of the time. That's perfectly normal. But compare the amount of time you spend each day thinking about yourself with the amount of time you spend thinking about others.

Do you study people?

To study people means to be really interested in them. I wonder if Anne is happy. I wonder if Joe is sad. I wonder what Sue is like. I'd really like to get to know each one of them.

We study so many things in life. We study so many subjects in school. We even study newspapers and television dramas. So much of what we study is geared to help us understand the people around us better. If we don't study the people around us, all the other study has gone to waste. It's like taking 99 steps to the refrigerator and not opening the door. It's like walking a mile for a Camel and then not buying any. It's like flying the Friendly Skies and staying on the plane when you get there.

* * * * *

So now you know some important things about people—that they are social, mysterious, influential, and interesting. This knowledge can certainly help you to encounter people in a truly human way, but it isn't enough, all by itself. There are certain dynamics involved, and certain skills to be mastered. To appreciate these, consider the problem of hitting a baseball. You can waste a lot of time and effort trying to become a good hitter, until you analyze what's happening. Basically, we have a cylinder (bat) meeting a sphere (ball). Since both have rounded surfaces, the way they meet is very important. The center of force of the bat must meet the center of mass of the ball. If they don't meet head-on, a great deal of energy is wasted. That's why the strongest players on the team aren't necessarily the best hitters. They may well be wasting much of their strength. In the same way, if you don't analyze a central dynamic involved in meeting people, you're going to waste a lot of energy.

To keep strikeouts and pop flies at a minimum in our lifelong game of human relations, let's examine the notion of mystery. Picture a cloud, with two ends of a rope coming out of it.

We pull down on the left-hand rope, and the rope on the right goes up. We pull on the right-hand rope, and the one on the left goes up. The two ends of the rope, of course, are connected in the middle, but we can't see the connection through the cloud as clearly as we'd like.

Many of the mysteries we meet have two ends with a connection we can't fully comprehend. There's a mystery in meeting people, too. And like other mysteries, it has two ends, with a connection that always eludes our grasp.

What are the two ends? Thanks to *God*, you encounter other people in your life. Thanks to you *yourself*, you encounter other people in your life. Both you and God are involved; without both of you, nothing happens.

You must see the hand of God in your life. It is God who in a mysterious way brings you close to others. Many a "chance" meeting results in a deep friendship. A person may be right under your nose every day for years. You look through each other, or settle for a nodding acquaintance. And then one day, mysteriously, you really *meet* that person. Thanks to God, you encounter other people.

Yet you're no puppet dangling from a string. You're a free, God-like person. You have to go out and seek the other, and you must be willing to receive the other. You must be receptive and ready to venture out, to leap toward the other. Thanks to yourself, you encounter other people.

If you just sit back and do nothing and say to God, "Okay, make it happen!"—forget it.

If you figure, "I don't need God, I can do it all by myself"— no way.

Thanks to God and thanks to you, encounters will happen.

* * * * *

So far, so good. And yet . . . .

We live in an evolving world. Because we humans exist in an evolving situation, neither you nor others are perfect. As a result, people encounters are filled with problems. To deal with these problems, we need certain skills. No one can give you those skills; you have to acquire them. But while we cannot give them to you directly, we can offer some guidance that will help you to acquire them.

Because of a lack of guidance, many people go through life with very few deep human encounters. Early in life they have a few unhappy encounter experiences and then decide to keep people at a distance for the rest of their lives. They don't want to get hurt again.

It's like a young child who tries to swim without help, swallows some water, gets discouraged, never learns to swim, and so misses out on a lot of fun.

Of course it's not the end of the world if you go through life without swimming. But you'll never realize a large part of your potential as a human being if you go through life with only a minimum of human encounters. As we discover: people need people.

* * * * *

That same lack of guidance, and maybe some bad early experiences, can also turn people off from Christianity.

What's the problem? Well, no one likes to play a game they can't win. And many people have convinced themselves that Christianity is a game you can't win. Often this is because they have a wrong idea of what a good Christian should be—namely, a doormat. To them, a good Christian is a person who always gives in and lets everyone walk all over him or her. Who wants to be a doormat? So they write off Christianity as a losing proposition, or a proposition for losers. They'd rather play a game where they can win.

They're wrong, of course. But when so many people get the same wrong impression, maybe it's because the Christians are doing something wrong. Maybe we should explain how being a Christian does *not* include being a patsy. To do this, we will also have to explain how to handle conflict, aggression, guilt, and rejection. For all these things happen when we try to relate to others. Things do go wrong between ourselves and others. How can we straighten them out?

In the next chapter we will examine the roots of conflict and how to handle conflict situations. There's no point in pretending that encountering other human beings is easy. Sometimes it's as hard and frustrating as hell. But we *have* to do it, and we *can* do it. The only sure way to avoid a flat tire in your travels is to leave your car in the garage. But then you'll never get anywhere. Why not take a spare and a jack? Whatsat? You don't know how to change a tire? So let us show you. Step this way, please. Welcome to our Human Encounter Accident Prevention and Repair Shop . . . .

Things to do
1. Read the poem *Richard Cory,* by Edwin Arlington Robinson. You will find it in any good American poetry anthology. Why do you think Richard killed himself?
2. Have you ever had a friend who helped bring out your good points?
3. Have you ever learned from experience that people are mysterious? Were you ever surprised to find a different side, or a new depth, in a person you thought you knew?
4. Pick out someone you see quite often—a classmate, an adult, a friend—and study him or her. Get beneath the surface. What is that person thinking, feeling? What makes them tick? What is he or she really like?
5. If you don't mind being a bit negative . . . . Pick out one sad story in your life—one human encounter that turned out badly. What happened? What went wrong? How did it affect you? Does the memory linger on?

CHAPTER 6

Repairs

WHAT TO DO WHEN THINGS GO WRONG

May 8, 1980

Human relations, like coins, have two sides. On the one hand, you have to respect the feelings, opinions, and rights of other people. On the other, you have your own feelings, opinions, and rights. When people can't make it together, it usually means that one or other side of the coin is being overemphasized or neglected. They have failed to strike a balance.

How do you strike a balance? There's no one answer for every case, but it's helpful to analyze what happens to two typical people.

Henrietta Hardnose is so wrapped up in her own feelings, so wedded to her own ideas, and so determined to protect her rights and "get her share" that she often rides roughshod over other people's emotions and interests. Selfish people do this a lot. Often the problem is not as serious as selfishness; it's simply thoughtlessness. Of course, if Henrietta is *habitually* thoughtless and inconsiderate, she's probably selfish.

Jerry Jellyfish has the opposite problem. He nearly always gives in. He wants everyone to be happy, and for him this means avoiding conflict. Happiness, for Jerry, is a world not only without war but without harsh words. He'll buy peace at any price. And if the price goes as high as ignoring his own emotions and legitimate interests, even sacrificing his own convictions, he'll pay without complaining. To him, everybody's feelings are important except his own.

In the next few pages, we'll meet several conflict situations which give the Henriettas and the Jerries of this world a lot of static. If we can avoid making the mistakes of these two losers, we can win in the game of human relations. Here are ten simple rules to remember:

1. It's okay to get mad.
2. 6 A.M. and 6 P.M. anger don't count.
3. Hate the sin but love the sinner.
4. Some skins are thinner than others.
5. Open all boxes and release people.
6. Bullies leave bruises.
7. Loving isn't the same as liking.
8. Don't trust first impressions.
9. After breakup, don't fall apart.
10. With too much rope, you can hang yourself.

1. *It's okay to get mad.*

Anger is justified at times, and should not leave us feeling guilty. Some parents get very uptight because they get angry at their children, but this may be just what the little darlings need. (On the other hand, parents shouldn't make the kid a punching bag for their emotional therapy.) We don't advise you to go around hitting everyone over the head with righteous anger, but it's good to know that you're not necessarily in the wrong just because you're angry.

Even Jesus Christ used to get angry sometimes. That simpering, meek-and-mild label some people hung on him was a bum rap. The ears of some scribes and pharisees are probably still burning from the way he told them off. And he didn't always limit himself to angry words, either. John Wayne in his best barroom brawls didn't do much more damage than Jesus did when he drove the buyers and sellers out of the Temple.

2. *6 A.M. and 6 P.M. anger don't count.*

It may happen that our anger isn't justified, but before we know it, it has sneaked out. Have you ever noticed that when you're tired or have things on your mind, anger can explode before you realize what's happening?

This is sometimes called "6 A.M. anger." Some people don't wake up human. They operate on an animal level until the morning coffee returns them to the human race. It is also known as 6 P.M. anger. Father is trying to unwind from the job. Mother has all the home problems that have been piling up all day. There's a meal to prepare. Everyone is hungry and tense . . . . Explosion! 6 P.M. anger.

By knowing the critical times, we can anticipate and defuse a certain amount of anger. But even if the blowup occurs and hard words are spoken, we can have sense enough not to take them too seriously.

3. *Hate the sin but love the sinner.*

If we analyze our feelings toward most people, we usually find two sets of emotions—positive and negative. Everyone around us has some defects, and these naturally annoy us. At the same time, we have good feelings toward the same person. What to do? Well, if you can direct the negative feelings toward the defects, and the positive feelings toward the person, you'll be able to like people without being dishonest or closing your eyes to truth.

Jesus used to operate this way. No one ever saw more deeply than he into people's real selves. Yet his love for them was without limits. He never denied the reality of sin nor made believe that evil didn't exist. He didn't look at life or at people with rose-colored glasses. He saw it and told it like it was. Yet underneath all their meanness, pettiness, and even malice, he saw what was there and loved what he saw.

4. *Some skins are thinner than others.*

Some people react quickly and forget just as quickly. They like to call a spade a spade. Anything inside them, out it comes. If they're dealing with someone who's just like them, fine—let it all pour out. There'll be a big explosion, but the smoke will clear away in no time.

Others react slowly and don't forget quickly. They have long memories, and hard words stay with them a long time. When dealing with this type of person, you can still tell it like it is, but *how* you do it is very important. It does no good to say that people shouldn't be sensitive; you can't argue with facts. Treating everybody the same may sound like a good idea, but it breaks down in the real world of real people who insist on being different.

5. *Open all boxes and release people.*

Someone once said, "Every time I see my tailor, he measures me again." We all have the tendency to type a person, put that person in a box, and never give him or her a chance to get out. People *can* change and want to try. But if they feel you have put them in a box and are sitting on the lid, they can get discouraged. And change, which is rarely easy, gets that much harder.

Jesus had a rare quality that made people around him feel good about themselves and their own possibilities. Sinners were encouraged to turn themselves around, and ordinary people rose to greatness. Because he believed in them, they could believe in themselves.

6. *Bullies leave bruises.*
The more you give in to a certain type of bully, the more he or she is going to demand. We think that by giving in we solve the problem. It only gets worse. This bully will back down only if you stand up to him or her. Remember Hitler?

Okay, so you stand up to the bully and what happens? After meeting him or her head-on, you feel crummy and upset. You say to yourself that your conscience is hurting you. I could feel this way only if I did something wrong. Most likely it's not your conscience at all; it may be a psychological black-and-blue mark.

There you are scoring the winning touchdown, banging head-on into that would-be tackler as you cross the goal line. You scored the touchdown (hurrah!), but in the process you picked up a bruise that's going to hurt you for some time.

When you bang into a bully, you can expect to pick up a few emotional bruises. Don't confuse these with your conscience.

7. *Loving isn't the same as liking.*
What's this stuff about loving everyone? There are too many people who bug the hell out of me. How can I pretend I love them, when they drive me right up the wall? You mean I have to go around with a loving feeling, a warm, tender emotion for everyone? No way!

No, you don't have to do the impossible. And it's impossible to *like* everyone. But it's not impossible to *love* everyone. What's the difference? Well, liking is something you do with your emotions; loving is something you do with your will. What you do with your will is far more important than what you do with your emotions. For we'll always have a very limited control of our feelings, which sometimes live a life of their own, quite apart from and often contrary to our real selves.

We're not saying feelings are unimportant. Ideally, we love not only with our will but also with warm, tender emotion—with all our powers. But sometimes we can love only with our wills. And this is no mere substitute for the real thing. Some of the greatest loving in the world has been done just with the will.

Take, for example, a husband who gets sick and is approaching delirium. The wife is nursing him. It's all very romantic in the beginning. He's near delirium, however, and his demands are out of this world. The soup is too hot. The soup is too cold. Go away and leave me alone. Where is everybody? Nobody stays with me. And so it goes. Around the end of the second day she doesn't have a warm, tender emotion in her body—but she continues to take care of him. In her emotions, it's grumble, grumble. In her will, in her heart, she loves him with a great love.

8. *Don't trust first impressions.*
Human emotions are funny things. Sometimes they're uncanny in their accuracy; other times they're unreliable indicators of how relationships are going to develop. We shouldn't fear our emotions or deny them. Rather, we should try to find their source and then deal with them. *Why* does so-and-so turn me on (or off)? Maybe for very good reasons; maybe for no reason at all. Feelings should be respected, but they're not infallible.

Consider the next fifty people you're going to meet for the first time. A couple of them you will take a shine to, right from the beginning. A couple of them will turn you off right away, maybe for no reason at all. There you are. Number One and Number Two can do no wrong; Forty-nine and Fifty can do no right. And Number Three to Forty-eight fall somewhere in the middle. After a while, some funny things happen. You really get to like old Forty-nine and Fifty when you get to know them.

Some first impressions, of course, are lasting. But it's wise to keep open to the possibility of a change of heart. There's so much more to people than meets the eye! And remember, you may well be someone's Number One and someone else's Number Fifty.

9. *After breakup, don't fall apart.*
You're dating. You're going steady. Suddenly, before you realize what's happened, you and your steady have broken up. Maybe you feel very sad. A breakup like that can really tear you up.

It's okay to feel sad at a time like this. The trouble is, there's a serious danger of infection from this wound. You can catch a bad case of inferiority feelings. This happens many times. You feel washed up. I guess I have no sex appeal. No one will ever be interested in me. My life plan just went down the drain. I'll never get married now. Etc., etc., etc.

Diagnosis: Incipient inferiority complex.

Prognosis: Bad times ahead, unless treated immediately.

Prescription: Sadness, yes; feelings of inferiority, no.

Why shouldn't we allow the breakup of a "steady" relationship to trigger an inferiority complex? Because then we miss the whole point of the dating game. What are the players in this game doing, anyway? You and they are meeting a variety of people and learning how to get along with one another, with the purpose of eventually making an intelligent choice of a marriage partner. A few marry their first boyfriend or girlfriend; most settle down with Number Four or Eight or Ten. There's no hard and fast rule.

Some very young people go exclusively steady too early in the game. There are two reasons for this. First, going steady is a status symbol. It tells the crowd I've arrived. Second, it's a hassle to find another steady and go through all the awkward preliminaries of meeting someone new.

Suppose the next raincoat you buy would be the last one you could ever have. You'd have to wear it for the rest of your life. You'd be very careful, checking out many stores before making a choice. You certainly wouldn't run into the first store and grab the first one you liked. And remember, this coat is only for *rainy* days!

It's good to know that God is very interested in you as you play the dating game. It means you're not alone.

10. *With too much rope, you can hang yourself.*

Growing up presents its own problems of getting along with others, especially between parents and older children.

When a child is born, it is 100 percent dependent and zero percent independent. It can't do anything by itself. Eating, drinking, moving about—all depend on others. Now gradually, as the child grows up, it can do certain things for itself—eat, drink, move about. Later the child can reason, accept certain responsibility, and make certain judgments. This continues until the young person matures into adulthood. Independence is gradually going from zero to 100 percent. The young adult has attained 100 percent independence, but his or her amount of life experience is still very limited. But this will increase as one goes through life.

The baby, the child, the teen-ager is constantly saying

"Now." *Now* I am ready to be on my own. The parent is constantly saying "Not yet—I don't think you're ready yet."

Parents can get out of this problem in either of two ways. They can lock their brains and sit on the growing person in every way. Everything is *not yet*, and it's never going to change. The result is a 21- year-old child with no confidence at all, or a runaway to parts unknown.

Or they can escape in the other direction. They can shut their eyes and turn the youth loose. Anything goes. Everything is *now*, right from the beginning. The end product is a 21-year-old spoiled child. There is also the possibility that such young people will panic while growing up. They have been told that everything is *now*. It's wide open. In their heart of hearts they know there have to be some limits. In order to find those limits, they do one crazy thing after another. And each one is worse than the one before it. In their panic they keep pushing out and out and out, looking for the limit. If they're lucky enough to have someone blow the whistle on them, they may sulk. But deep down they experience a sense of peace now that they know some acceptable limits, and their panic decreases.

Okay, so we have dependence constantly decreasing and independence constantly increasing. We have *now* on one side and *not yet* on the other. What to do? The name of the game, of course, is balance. It's more easily said than done. Why? Because the dependence-independence ratio is constantly changing. Six months ago, now, six months from now—all different. You're trying to balance a moving target.

Not only that. The rate of dependence-independence doesn't change at a steady speed. There are periods in the life of a child or teen-ager when the rate of change suddenly speeds up. So you can't sit down with your computer and figure out ahead of time exactly how much dependence or independence will be just right six months from now.

Moreover, every child or teenager is different. Even within the same family. One is reckless or overconfident. You have to pull back on him or her a bit. Another has no confidence. You have to let him or her go.

There are no concrete answers in this section. If, however, the teen-ager or parent who reads this begins to get an overview of an inherently difficult situation which calls for sensitivity and patience, we're making progress.

And if the teen-ager or parent begins to suspect that he or she needs God's help in all this, then this section has served its purpose.

* * * * *

The above ten rules, if remembered and followed, will help us to cope with most of the tensions and conflicts that threaten to undermine our efforts to encounter and relate to others in friendship and love.

Sometimes, though, the tensions are aggravated, misunderstandings multiply, and conflicts get beyond our control. Limited or total wars break out. When we try to patch things up and make peace again, we may find it difficult to get something better than a cease-fire or an uneasy truce. That's when we need not preventives but cures. Those ten rules came under the heading of Preventive Medicine. The following three are offered as possible cures, or better, Roads to Reconciliation:
1. Be ready to settle for 45 percent.
2. Go to a neutral corner, but don't stay there.
3. Let God put Humpty-Dumpty together again.

1. *Be ready to settle for 45 percent.*
Ideally, life should be a 50-50 proposition, where everyone gets a fair shake and people meet one another half way and no one gets the short end of the stick. Maybe in a finished world or in a static universe, things could work that way, but not in the present human condition. We live in an evolving universe, and we have to come to terms with it. That means being willing to give 55 percent and being happy to get 45. In settling for less than an even break, we're not just being nice guys; we're allowing for that margin of error which is necessary for evolution. This is realism in the best sense of the word.

2. *Go to a neutral corner, but don't stay there.*
Wow, what a fight! It might be a good idea if both of you would go to a neutral corner for a short time until you both calm down. Maybe you should skip talking for a time until you both feel better; you both need time to cool off. What matters here is timing. If you stop talking for too long, you could make the situation worse. You

might both want to talk again, but neither wants to be first to break the ice. First one who talks loses. So, a little quiet, please, but not too long.

3. *Let God put Humpty-Dumpty together again.*
If you think Henry Kissinger worked hard bringing people together, you should see God. The following is a good example of his work:

(Jack and Jill have had a fight. Enter God.)
God: Jack, any chance of making up with Jill?
Jack: No way.
God: You won't make up with Jill for her sake?
Jack: Negative.
God: Well, would you just get together with Jill for my sake and see what happens?
Jack: Well (grumble, grumble), okay.
(Same action takes place between God and Jill.)

God's hope is that eventually they'll make up not only for his sake but for each other's.

After the fight is over, it's possible that your friendship will turn out stronger and deeper than before. When you cut yourself, the skin parts, and it's painful. But when it comes together again and heals, the scar tissue is stronger than the normal skin. This can also happen with the friendship of two people. It's wise to remind ourselves of this possibility, lest we assume that friendship must always be weakened by conflict. With God's help, not only can we put Humpty-Dumpty together again; sometimes he can actually turn out better than before.

* * * * *

If we ended this chapter here and closed our Human Relations Repair Shop for the day, we could give you the wrong impression. You might leave thinking that conflict, expressed in anger, was the biggest or the only barrier to encounter and love. As a matter of fact, there's another problem that may occur, and it's more subtle and goes much deeper.

What's the opposite of love?
Anger?
Wrong.

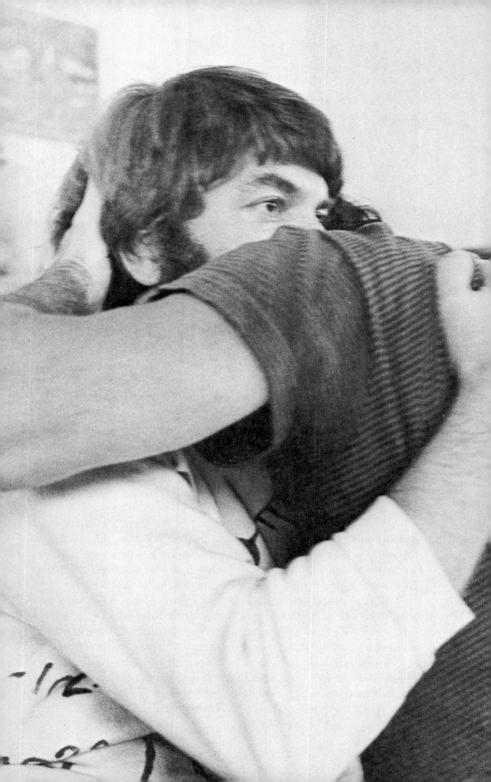

It isn't the best thing in the world, but it isn't the worst, either. Anger, paradoxically, is often tied up with love. "I thought you loved me. I thought that at least you'd respect my rights or my feelings. I counted on you, and you let me down."

Sometimes, even when we say we hate a person, what we're really saying is something like this: "I want you to suffer, at least a little bit. Not for the sake of suffering, but just so you'll understand what you did to me, how you made me feel."

Although at first sight anger seems to be 180 degrees removed from love, it's really at an angle.

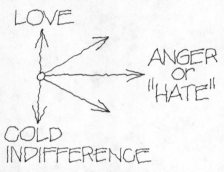

The direct opposite of love, the thing that's really terrifying, is cold indifference. "I'm absolutely not interested in you. I'm not angry at you. I don't hate you. I couldn't care less. Your existence or non-existence is of no concern to me at all."

If someone is angry at you or "hates" you, remember, it could be worse. He or she could simply not give a damn.

When you're on the receiving end of indifference, there isn't much you can do, at least on a one-on-one level. When groups or institutions are indifferent to you, you can try to attract attention — wave your arms, march, picket, demonstrate, set plastic bombs. But these methods don't work in one-on-one situations.

What you *can* do is check yourself out and make sure *you* aren't the one who hits others with cold indifference. Can it happen? Sure. It's very easy to be indifferent to the problems of others as long as I don't have to experience what they experience.

Some good things aren't important as long as *I* have them. Meanwhile, I don't appreciate the situation of a person who doesn't have them. Only when I'm deprived of them do I realize how very important ordinary things become.

I break a leg. Before, I didn't think much about my leg. Now I think about it all the time. I sprain my thumb. I used to take my right hand for granted. Not now.

I lose my wallet in a strange city. Suddenly money becomes very important. For some reason, I haven't had a meal in two days. Food has become the most important thing in my life.

Someone comes up behind me and puts his hand over my nose and mouth, and I can't breathe. After a few seconds, the most precious thing in the world is good old common air.

It's so easy to be indifferent to the problems of others. Only if I've had a similar experience can I fully appreciate what's happening to the other. But I can try to put myself in his or her place. I can try to be sensitive to other people's feelings, to imagine how it must be in their situation. I probably won't succeed completely (there's no substitute for experience), but that doesn't matter. All I have to do is try. And in trying, I escape the bottomless pit of self-centeredness, the quicksand of apathy. For now I care . . . and a funny thing happens. Suddenly, all kinds of people seem to care about me.

It works. No kidding. Try it and see.

Things to do
1. Take the Ten Rules. Rank the top five in order of importance. Give reasons for ranking them this way.
2. In your own life—or the life of someone you know—have you ever seen one of the three reconciliation principles work? Or a time when one of them *could* have worked?
3. From literature or observation or experience, tell of a case in which someone inflicted pain, not by anger or hatred, but by indifference.

CHAPTER 7

Detour

GOD IS NOT A BLOB

For the last few chapters, we've been learning about people—what they're like, what makes them tick, how we can better relate to them. And maybe we learned a few things about ourselves.

By this time, you know a lot about encountering others. That's one half of religious experience. The other half—encountering God—isn't so very different. The same rules that make for healthy human relationships—keeping our antennas out, being willing to take scary leaps, building campfires of love—apply to the way we meet and come to know and love God. And yet there are obstacles which may keep us from encountering God and achieving union with him. By the same token, if we can recognize these obstacles and overcome them, we may go a long way toward finding not only ourselves and other people but also the God who loves us, gives us life, and brings us together.

Before we tell you what those obstacles are, let us tell you about how a group of scientists once dealt successfully with a problem surprisingly like our own.

Years ago, physics was a very neat and orderly science. There was a place for everything, and everything in its place. Only one small problem remained: the view provided by this physics didn't quite correspond to reality. As orderly and complete as it was, it didn't quite reflect the real thing. Then one day somebody decided to look at the foundation of this physics, namely the atom.

The atom had been considered the absolute basic. In constructing reality, this is what you began with. This was the starting point, what everyone took for granted.

"Suppose," somebody suggested, "this is not the most basic thing. Suppose we have to go deeper to find the starting point." And that was the big breakthrough that sparked the discovery and the exploration of the whole world of sub-atomic reality. Besides radically transforming the world we live in, this discovery made a lot of physics text books go out of print, but it was worth it.

In viewing the cultural Christian (one born a Christian in a Christian environment), we've often considered certain notions to be absolutely self-evident starting points. One of these unchallenged notions has been that the cultural Christian loves God. This is often considered to be as basic as the atom once was; but like the atom theory, it holds up only so long as you don't examine it too closely.

As a matter of fact, although not many cultural Christians are *against* loving God, many of them don't do much of it, and some don't do it at all! Maybe it's not the basic starting point we thought it was. Perhaps we should look inside the "atom" of loving God. When we do, we find there the three obstacles we were looking for: 1) the Soul God, 2) the Absorbing God, and 3) the Faith God. Let's look at each of them more closely.

The Soul God

We can take you, put you in a big pot, and melt you down to a few minerals. As mineral, you're worth about two dollars (maybe a little more, with inflation). As mineral, you're not too interesting. Like a vegetable, you take in food and grow. As vegetable, you're ho-hum. As animal, you move around. We might go to the zoo to see you. But as a human person, you're really interesting.

Now let's look at interesting you—just what are you? "You are body and soul," someone says. And what is your soul? Why, everyone knows that. It's a little white cloud inside your chest. If you're bad, it turns black, and if you're sorry, it turns white again. When you die, it drifts up to the big cloud in the sky where we put a bed sheet over it (wings optional), give it a harp, and let it live happily ever after. Dullsville!

Do we have any idea what the soul is really like? Perhaps the easiest explanation is to say that the soul is *you*. The soul is your alive-ness. The soul is your interesting-ness. The soul is your free will. It is the deepest source of your ability to live, to grow, to love and to be loved. It makes your body move, turns your emotions on. It's you thinking. The soul is that wonderful "I" that you keep calling yourself. Your soul is *you*!

As we try to understand the you-soul, let's not lose sight of the you-body. We might start to think of your body as some kind of overcoat that you put on and take off. No way! You're not an angel or some kind of spirit. You're human, and you're one. You don't come in two sections like a suit of clothes—jacket and pants. You're one. Your body is *you*!

Rather than refer to you as body and soul, or as a piece of this and a piece of that, rather than split you down the middle, let's just refer to *you*—the you that's an interesting person.

What's the point of all this? The point is that God is the God of *you* and not the God of your soul. He wants to relate to you as a whole, as a person, and not just to some so-called segment of you. God doesn't have a split vision of you: an important part (soul), a less important part (body). Nor does he have a split vision of your life (a religious part, a non-religious part). He wants to relate to the whole you and to the whole of your life. He's not only the God of the prayer, the Church, the Mass. He's also the God of the dance, the bus, the fight-with-my-mother, the game.

Unfortunately, many people have a split vision of themselves. As a result, they relate only to a "God-of-the-soul," who is spooky, severe, dull, and boring. These same people usually have a split vision of their lives. As a result, they relate only the so-called "religious" part of their lives to God; he's like company who's allowed in only when the house is clean.

The Absorbing God

A little earlier, while looking at the big picture of an evolving universe, we saw how, over billions of years, God gradually produces his masterpiece: mineral becomes vegetable, vegetable becomes animal, animal becomes human.

Besides this long, imperceptibly slow progress up the ladder of life, there's also a kind of instant evolution going on right under our noses. Look at this apple tree. "Not very exciting," you say? But look closer. The tree is using its roots to absorb minerals from the ground. What was mineral a short time ago has now become part of a tree, and hence vegetable in the broad sense.

Along comes a cow and eats one of the apples. What was originally dirt became vegetable and is now part of an animal.

The day comes when the farmer feels like having a nice steak. Good-bye, cow. Now what was originally dirt has gone through the vegetable and the animal kingdoms and has become part of a human.

It's a kind of poor person's evolution. What's significant is the *upsurge*. Whether it's the universe evolving over billions of years or the analogous phenomenon of instant evolution, the message is the same—an ascent to a higher form of life. In this ascent is a great destiny for the human; for the human too is upsurging and encountering God. Lower levels of life can't bear such an intimate encounter with a higher form of life without disastrous results. Humans, however, are at an evolutionary height where they not only can bear such an encounter but are even enhanced by it.

Yet perhaps the human race still carries a residual "memory" (or hangover?) of an earlier and lower place on the scale of life where it was safer to stay away from higher levels of life. It's interesting that the elements sodium, potassium, and calcium are in our bloodstream in almost the same proportion as they are in sea water. We received this makeup from one of our earliest ancestors on the scale of life when it had merely sea water in its circulatory system. (See Rachel Carson, *The Sea around Us*, pages 14-15.) And there's still a residual trace of a third eye inside our skulls, also bequeathed to us from some remote ancestor.

Just as we retain these inheritances from earlier and lower forms of life, perhaps we also carry within us a certain nameless fear of meeting a higher level of existence. This might explain why many people feel threatened by God. They acknowledge that God is good, but they want to keep a certain distance between themselves and him. There's the unspoken fear that if he gets too close (or if, perish the thought, they should get "spiritual" and thus too close to him), their humanity, their personality, their individuality will suffer.

If they could put this unspoken fear into words, they might say something like this:

> Let's go back to that upsurge for a minute. Look what happened to the apple. Sure, it met with a higher form of life, but it got eaten to death in the process. Look what happened to the cow. It met with a higher form of life, all right, but in the process it got it right between the eyes.
>
> Do you know what's going to happen to us if we meet with God? We'll meet with a higher form of existence, but in the process we're going to get it— probably between the eyes. Oh, we won't get killed.

> But we're going to end up like some kind of religious zombies. You know—real squares, really out of it, no personality. Life will be oh so righteous, but dull, dull, dull.
>
> Remember those science-fiction movies, where they invent this blob in the laboratory, and it breaks free? The next thing you know, it's rolling down the street and absorbing everything in its path. Maybe God's like a spiritual blob that'll just roll over us and swallow up our individuality and leave just a great big zero.

The above may well be the feeling of many people although they've never actually put it into words. God doesn't act that way. In fact, there's a tremendous breakthrough in his evolutionary masterpiece when it gets to the human level. Up until the human level, as we've seen, each level loses its own identity when it meets with a higher level. Not so with us. When the human level meets with the higher level (God), identity is not lost. In fact, just the opposite happens. The human is enhanced. It becomes more human. The person becomes more of a person, the individual becomes more of an individual. Far from being swallowed up, one's humanity, personality, and individuality are increased.

Know yourself. Listen to that something in your heart of hearts that's more basic than your heartbeat. Know your destiny, which is upsurge. Recognize your innate fear for what it is, the unfounded anxiety that you may lose your identity. And acknowledge your potential, which is nothing less than fulfillment through encounter with God—a fulfillment far beyond your wildest dreams.

We get a foretaste of this when we receive Holy Communion. We worry about meeting this God who is going to cramp our style. We worry about being absorbed by some higher form of life. And yet here is God coming to us under the appearances of bread. We could say vegetable, but, to all intents and purposes, under the appearance of a mineral form. Certainly not very threatening. Maybe he knows how threatened we feel.

It's interesting that when you receive Christ's resurrected body in Communion, you receive the pledge that even though death means a downsurge to the mineral level, God is going to resurrect you in a way that will knock your eye out.

The Faith God

Nostalgia takes many forms. High school juniors, who aren't very old, sometimes reminisce about the Good Old Days: "Boy, I had such great faith when I was in the seventh grade! But ever since then, it's been all downhill."

As you grow up, you become less dependent on older people for your ideas, your values, and your convictions. From this you could get the impression that faith, for you, is a thing of the past and plays no part in your young adult life. But faith is essential to all aspects of life, not just to religion. In an evolving universe, it's an essential ingredient for all human activity.

Did you ever stop to think how many times a day you use faith? Not just in religion. All the time.

Suppose you had *no faith at all*. Look at what would happen:

The radio announcer says the exact time is four P.M. (Nope. I don't believe you.)

The TV shows pictures of a flood in Canada. (How do I know that's Canada? How do I know there *is* a Canada? I've never been there.)

A book tells me Washington crossed the Delaware. (Washington's a myth. There *is* no Delaware River, because I've never seen it.)

A newspaper informs me that A beat B in a tennis match in Mexico City. (There *is* no such person as A. Ditto for B. And the same goes for Mexico City!)

A sign says the bridge one mile down the road has fallen into the river. (No way, say I, as I press down on the accelerator.)

"I'm never going to get on a bus or train again because I can't trust the driver. How do I know he'll stop at my station?"

"I'm never going to eat again. How do I know the food isn't poisoned?"

"I'm never going to listen to anybody again. I'll pour concrete into my ears, because you can't believe anybody."

"I'm turning off my own mind because I can't relate to anyone or anything. This is me signing off . . . . "

The only way to be "safe" would be to get inside a safe and stay there. "Zero faith" means a very narrow, neurotic life. In fact, it means no life at all.

So faith is not just something in the religious scene; it applies to every aspect of our lives. All life is a gamble, a risk, an adventure, a leap. No gamble, no risk = no faith = no life. Whether in relation to God or to others, it's only when we're willing to take the gamble and run the risk that life and happiness begin.

So what ever happened to that wonderful faith you had in the seventh grade? Maybe it fell victim to the classic difficulty of the cultural Christian. You know what we mean by a cultural Christian—someone who's born into a Christian family, brought up in the Church and taught the Christian religion, without ever going through a process of personal conversion. (In other words, no Stages 1 through 6.)

The problem is that the cultural Christian, to a certain extent, does things bass ackwards.

Consider for a moment how children learn their native language. First they speak the language; much later, they learn the grammar. Because they follow a natural order of learning, they are able to *communicate* well (though perhaps not in a grammatically correct fashion) in their native language. Quite different is the case of adults who take up a second language. Depending on the method of instruction, they may find themselves concentrating on the grammar rules rather than on the actual speaking of the language. As a result, while they may be grammatically correct, they don't communicate well with others in this language. You can probably verify this from your own experience, especially if you've studied a foreign language in high school. French or German grammar can tie you up in knots, and speaking those languages may come very hard. How much easier it was to learn English! You were talking a blue streak before anybody even told you about grammar, because you learned the natural way.

Well, there appears to be a "natural" order in the faith encounter with God, too. When it's reversed, as happens sometimes with the cultural Christian, the person may be technically correct about the many "somethings" involved—the doctrines, the laws, the Bible stories—but may not communicate well with the "Someone" involved. Such a person knows the prayers, the right words, the gestures, but has no *feel* for it. He or she has mastered the "grammar" of religion but can't communicate. And without communication—without encounter—religion is just words, words, words.

Put it another way: You normally believe *someone* before you believe *something*. You're reluctant to believe what strangers tell you, especially in matters of importance. If that stranger becomes an acquaintance, you may find it a little easier to take his or her for something. But if a deep friendship gradually develops between you, your willingness to believe this person is greatly increased. The closer you get to someone, the more you are able to believe the something he or she tells you.

Now look at the experience of a person who is not born a Christian but is converted to the faith as a teen-ager or adult. At first God is a stranger. Who can believe a stranger? Then someone or some event introduces them to God, who becomes a casual acquaintance. Gradually an intimate friendship develops with a personal God. Now the person believes Someone and is prepared to believe something on his word.

It's only when a newcomer has an experience of a personal God that things start to happen. One encounters God, believes God, and then believes what God says.

Now look at the experience of many American Christians. We're baptized as infants. As we grow up, there seems to be an overemphasis on the many somethings we're to believe, and the Someone gets lost. We know a lot of religion, but we've never really met God.

What to do now? Are we messed up for life? Nope. What we have to do now is see if we can have an encounter with the Someone.

Hello, operator. Give me God, please.

* * * * *

Once we've gotten over our hangups with the Soul God, the Absorbing God, and the Faith God, we may be ready for real faith through a real encounter with the real God. At this point, it's time to remind you that faith between you and God is very much like a marriage. If he wants to get married but she doesn't, no marriage. If she's ready but he isn't, those wedding bells won't chime. Faith is the same: it takes two.

God takes a shine to you. He makes an approach and opens himself to you. But you'll have none of it. Result: no faith encounter. God isn't going to put a gun to your head. But he finds you very interesting, and he'll probably try again, for he thinks a lot of you. But no guns. He doesn't want you unless you're free.

On the other hand, you can't arrive at a faith encounter all by yourself. Remember the spiritual weightlifter syndrome? "I'm going to work this whole thing out by myself." It doesn't work that way. If God doesn't give himself to you, nothing happens.

It takes two for a friendship. It takes two for a marriage. It takes two for a faith encounter.

It's nice to know that even when we're not ready, God is always ready and willing to encounter us. That doesn't mean we should take him for granted, just that he's more patient with us than we are with ourselves.

He's ready. Are you?

Things to do
1. *The Soul God*. What is meant by the "Soul God"? How does such an idea of God make it hard to love him? How can this wrong idea be corrected?
2. *The Absorbing God*. It is an undeniable fact that when some people become religious, they also become creepy. Does it have to be this way? Do you know any people whom religion has made more interesting and alive? Did their idea of God make a difference?
3. *The Faith God*. Point out three times you have acted on faith in the last 24 hours.
4. What is a cultural Christian? Why is faith in God a problem for such a person?

CHAPTER 8

On Our Way

FACE TO FACE

We spent most of the last chapter clearing away the underbrush, removing the artificial obstacles and misunderstandings that keep us from encountering God. Now that we've disposed of the Soul God, the Blob God, and the Faith God, will the real God please stand up? No, that's the wrong question. He's been standing up all the while. The question is, Are you ready to stand up to him? Are you willing to encounter the real God?

If you are, then in a real sense this book is working for you. In fact, you may be even further along than that. In the course of reading and using this book, doing the exercises, seeking and sharing and taking chances, you may have already *experienced* to some extent what we've been talking about. By this time, God may have become for you more than a word, more than a rumor started by someone else; he may already be part of your own personal, private world.

If it hasn't happened yet, but if you're still open to the experience of meeting the living God, let's talk about what happens when we encounter him. What does it feel like? What are the dynamics involved in this most mysterious and profound of all relationships?

Even if you've already encountered him and your relationship is fairly well developed, this last chapter is for you. The more you understand about God and yourself and the inner workings of religious experience, the better chance you have of achieving close union with God and thus fulfilling to the limit your possibilities as a person.

*　*　*　*　*

How does it feel to encounter God? Well, of course, everyone is different, and no two people encounter or relate to God in exactly the same way. The possibilities and variations are limitless. Some experience God as simply *being with* them. There is a deep-down awareness of him as Presence—supporting, caring, consoling. For others, the encounter means feeling *called*. God has summoned me, and I have responded. There's the feeling that God made the first move, that before I chose God, he chose me. Why, I can't explain.

This doesn't mean that God loves me *instead* of others, or at their expense. No, he loved them, too. And yet there's something special about this presence, about this call. He has made a personal, individual, free choice of me. No matter how many people are involved, God doesn't choose people in bunches. He picks them one by one and by name.

On the other hand, just because God chose me doesn't mean that I'm the greatest thing around. Why did he pick me? Because I'm the best, or the most? Nope. Well then, why? So don't ask. Look, love is mysterious. The heart has its own reasons. Why do *you* love the people you do—because they're the handsomest, the smartest, the richest, the most talented? No, love doesn't work that way . . . thank God! So don't ask why God loves you. Respect the mystery, accept the fact in gratitude and awe.

There's another side to this experience. Not only is the person chosen by God; in a real sense, he or she chooses God, too. It takes two to make an encounter, to form a friendship, to seal a marriage. An encounter is based on love, and love is based on freedom. As God freely chooses us, so we freely choose God. This doesn't mean we're not scared. Ever watch the bridegroom at a wedding? He's trying to look cool, but nobody is fooled.

Once the person answers the call and chooses freely to respond, you might think that all is well. The wedding is over, and all that remains is to live together happily ever after. But in real life, marriages don't work that way; neither do friendships, and neither do relationships between ourselves and God.

Many people in their encounter with God find themselves in a bind. On the one hand, let's say you're hurting. God seems at times to be indifferent to you. It looks as though he's hiding, not returning your love. And so you feel angry. On the other hand, you're told that God is perfect, that he wears a white cowboy hat, and is all-good, all-just, all-merciful. So how can you get mad at a perfect God? There you are, stuck with your anger and your pain, and you're not even supposed to feel it.

Some people see the problem as insoluble and withdraw from all God relations. Others may not think the matter out so clearly. All they know is that over a period of time their relations with God have gone downhill.

To get out of this bind, we must admit the difference between 1) God as he is, and 2) God as I experience him.

God, as he is, is infinite and perfect. God as I experience him is far from perfect. In my limited fashion, the God that I know is a God who seems to hide himself, who seems to let me down on many occasions, who seems to be uninterested in me, who seems to keep his distance.

God, as I know him, doesn't exactly seem to be the greatest, and I ought to let him know about it. If I feel he's let me down, I should let him know how I feel about it—in spades. If I feel he's always hiding himself (and how can I love a God I don't know?), I ought to tell him so in no uncertain terms. It doesn't matter if my words aren't the finest. If a person I hardly know lets me down, well, I chalk it up to experience. But if I feel that someone I count on, someone I'm trying to love, someone I think loves me, ignores me and lets me down, I'm going to tell that person about it—and the words may not be nice.

This may be hard to do. It may violate an unspoken taboo deep within me. But what happens is that the boil is lanced; the anger, hurt, loneliness, frustration come forth, and there can be healing.

A much more important thing may also be happening. Perhaps for the first time in my life I'm relating to God as a Person and not as an abstraction.

Anger at God is not some new, shocking idea. The psalms, Bible hymns and poems written under God's inspiration, have many expressions of it. Many times the psalmist tells God just what he thinks of him.

The original language of the psalms, ancient Hebrew, dealt mostly in terms of black and white and didn't bother much with fine distinctions or shades of gray. So when the psalmist in the original Hebrew was mad at God, he was really mad! English, on the other hand, has many distinctions of gray. So when the psalms are translated into English, a more diplomatic language, they're toned down somewhat.

When you feel free enough to talk frankly to God, you're ready for a relationship that is not only vertical but also horizontal:

GOD
↑
↓
YOU ←——→ GOD

No matter how high an opinion you may have of yourself, you have to admit that God is greater than you. Hence you relate "up" to God. Yet if this is a love encounter, there's another relationship which we may term face-to-face. Lovers, no matter what their difference in rank (and this includes Creator-creature), also meet as equals. There's an equality to love that brings the two eye-to-eye, face-to-face. Thus, if a king or queen marries a commoner, their social rank in public may differ, but they come to each other on equal terms as husband and wife.

Encounterers, of course, relate "up" to God. At the same time, though, in meeting God they're relaxed and enjoy his company. They speak freely and don't worry about fancy words. They're not afraid to let God know, in plain language, when they feel let down. They relate to a God whom they love and who loves them: face-to-face. (Wouldn't this face-to-face relationship be tremendously enhanced if God were ever to become a human being?)

Face to face. One-on-one. I and thou. Do we really know God this way? Isn't his face obscure, hidden in shadows? Saint Paul, who was into mystical experience, wrote:

> What we see now is like a dim image in a mirror; then we shall see face-to-face. What I know now is only partial; then it will be complete—as complete as God's knowledge of me.

(1 Cor. 13:12 — Good News Bible)

Encounterers want God to reveal himself. They don't expect visions, but they realize that they can't love what they don't know. They know you can't begin to love someone unless you meet and experience that someone. And so they pray, "God, please reveal yourself to me. What are you like? Will the real God please stand up? What are your thoughts, your feelings, your experiences? What do you think of yourself? What are you really like? The philosopher tells me that you are the source of truth and goodness and beauty and love and life. That statement means nothing to me. I want to *experience* your goodness, your beauty, your truth, your love, your life. God, please reveal yourself to me, and continue to do so."

You want to *know* God—not just with your mind, but with your whole self. This is the knowledge of *union*. But union with God involves a mystery.

We have two ends of the mystery and a connection between them. We cannot clearly see the connection, but we understand it to some degree.

What are the two parts of this mystery called union with God?

The first part is that in this union you are continually entering deeper and deeper into the life of God. Now, your first reaction, on hearing something like this, is that this is just a pious or poetic statement. You know—a nice warm expression but with no real meaning, a kind of dynamic non-statement, a little pious whipped cream.

No way. In this union you are really entering into God's life; so much so, that we can truly say that you and God are one.

Did you ever notice how you want to hug someone you love? What you want to do is become one with that person. Even very young children hold out their arms to embrace and be embraced. They may not even be able to talk yet, but they know that desire to be one with the beloved.

The embrace, the being one, the union between you and God

is not just a hug of a few seconds. It's deeper and closer than you can possibly imagine. And it can grow deeper and closer every day.

The other part of the mystery is that you are you. You and God are one, and yet (mystery!) you are you. You are eternal. You will always be you. You are unique. There never was, there isn't now, nor will there ever be, another you. There's something special and interesting about you, simply because you are you. You are never going to be smothered, never going to be absorbed.

We can only hope to understand to some small degree the connection between the two parts of this mystery. Yet there you are. The intimate oneness between yourself and God is compatible with the fact that you are a unique person and always will be.

* * * * *

What lies ahead for you and God, as your friendship grows and deepens? And what can you do to nourish that relationship? How can you stay close?

Here are seven suggestions. Most of them apply to any human relationship and would help any friendship along. A few apply in a special way to our friendship with God.

1. *Try not to take God for granted*. Beware of the "sponge" gratitude that is really ingratitude. It's easy to absorb all the good things he gives us, and go our merry, thoughtless way. Jesus cured ten lepers, and only one came back to thank him. That's inexcusable.

If, like the one grateful leper, you remember to say thank you, don't do it in the spirit of "balancing the books." You know what we mean. Some of us don't like the idea of anyone, even God, being one up on us. Jesus tells this story about a pharisee praying in the Temple, "O God, I thank you that I am not like the rest of men. I fast . . . I give to charity . . . my books are balanced, Lord!"

To understand true gratitude, we must first understand what a gift is. A gift is a symbol of love. We can't *see* love, so we use symbols, like a wedding ring. When God gives us a gift, he's saying: "Here, I want you to have this. Enjoy it. See it as a symbol of my love for you." So true gratitude is returning love for love.

2. *Don't be afraid to ask him for things*. Don't be embarrassed. Ask for big things and little things. Ask for yourself and for others. Don't get uptight about asking for too much; it's impossible. With God there are no quotas, no items in short supply. Think big; ask for the large size. And don't get any hangups about asking

for "worldly" things. If it's important to you, he cares.

Of course, you know very well that you're not going to get everything you ask for. Some turn-downs you'll take in stride, but some will really hurt. Sometimes at a later date you'll be able to look back and see why you were better off not getting what you asked for. But sometimes you may never see why, at least not in this life. And no amount of theology is ever going to explain why.

3. *Share the pain*. When suffering comes, don't suffer in silence, and don't suffer alone. Don't try to handle life's setbacks all by yourself. Ask God to share the experience, to share the emotion with you. This goes especially for those crisis times, when the roof falls in on you and you feel you've been clobbered. At such critical moments, the academic statement that God can draw good from evil means nothing. Like a blind person, you can only cry out—perhaps not even in words—asking God to take your hand and lead you through.

(Thought: If God ever became a human being and experienced crises of his own, wouldn't he be better able to share mine?)

4. *Be alert to his presence all around you*. Does Nature turn you on? Do you like mountains, clouds, sun, and stars? These things are beautiful, and anyone can enjoy them. But when you encounter God, you also see them as gifts, gifts from God. You see God in a flower, in a snowflake, in a blade of grass. You look at a sunset, and you see a personal gift from God, who had you personally in mind. And then all the world becomes a church, when heaven and earth proclaim the glory of God, who gives them to you.

5. *Work with him*. Even if you'd rather play than work . . . even if your parents and teachers think you're lazy . . . even if your favorite daydream is an endless vacation, you know that you're going to work, and that you want it that way. Without a goal, without a project, without something to accomplish, you'd eventually get bored out of your skull.

Why is this drive so basic? Because you're a lot like God, who is always busy, busy, busy evolving his masterpiece, the universe, and the human race as part of it. And he wants your help. Not only are you called to evolve, but you're also called to play a role in helping God bring the world and the human race to completion.

Why does God want your help? Consider a father who wants to give a sailing ship model to his three-year-old son. He buys the model, assembles all the parts, and gives it to the child. The kid is happy, and that's nice. But here's another father who buys the same model ship for his little son. Instead of assembling the model by himself, he asks the boy to help, and *together* they build the ship. The little kid contributes maybe one percent of the work, the father the other 99 percent, but it's a moment of special delight when they can say, "Look at the ship *we* made! Look at *our* ship!"

It's the same with evolving the universe. The human race can't evolve the universe alone. Compared to God's, our contribution is small, yet it's vital; it makes all the difference in the world. Because of that contribution the universe is now *our* universe, and eventually it will become the masterpiece that *we* have evolved.

What does this mean for your daily life? It means that everything you do has a lasting effect. Wash the dishes, clean the floor, ride the bus, do your homework, cut the grass, open a textbook, sew on a button . . . each of these has more than an immediate effect like getting a house clean or passing a test or collecting a salary. It also has a lasting effect on the big work, *our* work of evolution.

You may not be famous. Your picture may not be in the paper. But you are vital. When you sweep a floor, you and God sweep it together. When you finish, the two of you not only have a clean floor. Both of you have moved the universe a little way toward fulfillment.

6. *Be with him*. Church is not the only place you can meet God and be with him. You can experience union with him in any situation.

Encounterers like to get together with God, whom they meet everywhere. At the department store, at the factory, on the train, in front of the TV set . . . all over the place they keep bumping into God. They walk alone, and they bump into God. When they bump into other people, they bump into God.

People who encounter are sharers. Anything interesting or pleasant that happens to them, they share with God. Encounterers are also "dumpers." Any problem at all, anything rotten that happens, they "dump" on God. They don't try to go it alone.

Encounterers are listeners. They listen to God everywhere. It's not that they expect any telephone calls from heaven. But they listen. And things do happen.

Encounterers like to get together with God. They like God's company. God feels the same way about them. And about you.

7. *Remember, he's getting a good deal, too*. It's true that God

doesn't *need* us, that he's perfect in himself. And we know we're far from perfect. Your faults certainly don't turn you on. But if you're becoming an encounterer, then by this time you should not only *love* yourself but even *like* yourself. And because you love yourself, you realize that you have value. In loving God, you try to share this value with him.

God loves you. That means he finds something beautiful and good when he looks at you. In meeting you, and in becoming friends with you, he thinks he's getting a good deal. Why argue with him? Sure, he knows your flaws and limitations. But he sees beyond these to the interesting you, to the you who can and will be—if you answer his call and stay close to him and to other people.

* * * * *

These are just a few helpful hints for you as you answer God's call to meet him and to be with him and others. No two people encounter God in exactly the same way, and your relationship with him will be special, even unique. Eventually you may get comfortable with each other. Until then, we're just glad to have had the privilege of introducing you.

Epilogue

How do you finish a book like this? If it worked for you, then we may have started something that literally will never end. If you were not content simply to read, but opened yourself to experience, you may now be embarked on an exciting voyage that in a real sense is only beginning. If you learned about yourself, tried to relate to others, and began to encounter God, then you have indeed taken the longest step. Unlike Charlie Brown, you had the courage to cross the schoolyard and to encounter the other. And you may have learned from experience the third law of evolution, that when things get together, things happen.

Bill and Joan, the two travelers, weren't actually engaged in world-shaking decisions. Whether to spend four weeks in Europe or in Hawaii is not, after all, a very crucial choice. But if you really went back to zero and tried to start your journey over . . . if you took the leap and the risk and went out to meet other people and God . . . then you were playing for high stakes. Are you glad you made the trip? Is the trip over, or is it just beginning?

Before you close this book and put it down for the last time, ask yourself three questions, and come up with some answers. It would be well to write down your answers in your journal.

1. Where were you when you started this book? How would you describe your feelings about yourself and your relations with others and with God?

2. Where are you now? Do you feel the same or differently about yourself? Are your relations with others and God the same or different? How?

3. In reading this book and in the experience growing out of it, has your life changed in any way? How?

4. Are these the right questions, or do you think others should be asked? If others, what are they? And what are your answers?

When we invited you on this trip, we were hoping to help you become your best self. We wanted you to start or continue a voyage of discovery—the lifelong journey of getting in touch with your deepest self, encountering others in love, and experiencing a love relationship with the living God. That's quite an order! Maybe it's too much to ask of a book or a course. But we consider ourselves matchmakers, who arrange a meeting, smooth the way, and hope for the best. We were and are convinced that, whatever the response on your part, God loves you dearly and looks forward to your love freely given in return—sometimes one-on-one with him, sometimes through love shared with other people.

In the one-on-one faith encounter with God, don't be surprised if you experience two very different feelings from time to time. At times a feeling of easiness, calm, and security will prevail. At other times, a sense of uneasiness, fear, and confusion will predominate. Just because the latter feeling is dominant, it doesn't mean your faith is weakening. In fact, it may mean just the opposite. It may be a sign that you're growing, that you're experiencing a deeper faith encounter.

If we have succeeded in helping you encounter God and other persons, then this point in your life marks both an end and a beginning. It's the end of the longest step and the beginning of a marvelous story whose outline is thrilling but whose details you can only dimly perceive. There are so many questions still unanswered. What role does Jesus play in this story? What, if any, part will a church community play? How do you relate to your personal spiritual history—the Church you grew up in, the religion you were taught, the prayers you've learned and said, the worship in which you've participated? And many, many others.

For now, however, we'll close with a word of sincere congratulation to you for whatever effort you put into reading and trying to live this book. Any time you level with yourself, open up to others, and sincerely seek after God, you've accomplished something very important and worthwhile. You may not see the results right away, but they'll surprise you. For now, it's enough to know that you've taken the first and longest step. You're no longer alone, and you're on your way.

Don't stop.

Photo Credits:
John Arms   25, 67, 82
Rohn Engh   76
Freda Leinwand   46, 70, 89
Jean-Claude Lejeune   12, 41, 49, 65
Richard Olsenius opposite   1, 17
Cyril A. Reilly   20
Rick Smolan   7, 32
Elizabeth Thoman   28
Vivienne   52, 56